¯_(ツ)_/¯

The MIT Press Essential Knowledge Series

A complete list of the titles in this series appears at the back of this book.

NIHILISM

NOLEN GERTZ

The MIT Press | Cambridge, Massachusetts | London, England

This book was set in Chaparral Pro by Toppan Best-set Premedia Limited. Printed and bound in the United States of America.

Library of Congress Cataloging-in-Publication Data

Names: Gertz, Nolen, author.
Title: Nihilism / Nolen Gertz.
Description: Cambridge, MA : MIT Press, 2019. | Series: The MIT Press essential knowledge series | Includes bibliographical references and index.
Identifiers: LCCN 2018043231 | ISBN 9780262537179 (pbk. : alk. paper)
Subjects: LCSH: Nihilism (Philosophy)
Classification: LCC B828.3 .G47 2019 | DDC 149/.8—dc23 LC record available at https://lccn.loc.gov/2018043231

10   9   8   7   6   5   4

CONTENTS

SERIES FOREWORD

The MIT Press Essential Knowledge series offers accessible, concise, beautifully produced pocket-size books on topics of current interest. Written by leading thinkers, the books in this series deliver expert overviews of subjects that range from the cultural and the historical to the scientific and the technical.

In today's era of instant information gratification, we have ready access to opinions, rationalizations, and superficial descriptions. Much harder to come by is the foundational knowledge that informs a principled understanding of the world. Essential Knowledge books fill that need. Synthesizing specialized subject matter for nonspecialists and engaging critical topics through fundamentals, each of these compact volumes offers readers a point of access to complex ideas.

Bruce Tidor
Professor of Biological Engineering and Computer Science
Massachusetts Institute of Technology

WHY DOES IT MATTER THAT NOTHING MATTERS?

"I Honor Nihilism"

On June 30, 1881, Wendell Phillips—a 70-year-old Massachusetts orator, writer, and abolitionist—gave a speech at Harvard University for the Centennial Meeting of the Phi Beta Kappa honor society. Phillips became famous for his oratory after he gave a passionate defense of the abolitionist movement in a speech at Boston's Faneuil Hall in 1837. In fact, Phillips became so well-regarded that soon after his death in 1884 a neighborhood in Minneapolis was named after him, schools in Chicago and Washington, DC, were named after him, awards at Tufts and Harvard were named after him, and a statue was erected of him in the Boston Public Garden. The statue boldly declares that Wendell Phillips was a "Prophet of Liberty" and a "Champion of the Slave."

Yet it was reported that the Phi Beta Kappa speech that Wendell Phillips gave in 1881 did not go over well with the honor society crowd. It was reported that it was "strange to Harvard ears—wicked and perverse."[1] The likely reason for this is that Phillips used the speech to make the following argument:

> Nihilism is the righteous and honorable resistance of a people crushed under an iron rule. Nihilism is evidence of life ... the last weapon of victims choked and manacled beyond all other resistance. It is crushed humanity's only means of making the oppressor tremble. ... I honor Nihilism since it redeems human nature from the suspicion of being utterly vile, made up of heartless oppressors and contented slaves. ... This is the only view an American, the child of 1620 and 1776, can take of Nihilism—any other unsettles and perplexes the ethics of our civilization.[2]

Today we might similarly find this speech strange, wicked, and perverse, even if we do not have "Harvard ears." For why would anyone not only *defend nihilism* but go so far as to argue that "the only view an American" can take on nihilism is that it is "righteous and honorable"?

While it might seem like it would help to clarify what Phillips was arguing to know that he was referring to the political movement in Russia that self-identified as "Nihilists," this fact really only makes this situation more confusing. The Russian Nihilists sought to overthrow what they saw as an oppressive and tyrannical regime, for which reason we can see why an abolitionist would support them. Yet their plan to achieve this aim was to destroy society as a whole in order to build a new society out of whatever survived their destruction. The Nihilists first attempted to destroy society by advocating for the destruction of social practices and traditional values, such as private property, marriage, and religion. But when mere advocacy didn't work, they turned to assassination, trying several times to assassinate Tsar Alexander II, which they finally succeeded in doing on March 13, 1881, or just over three months before Phillips's speech.

What we mean by nihilism in everyday usage and what the Russian Nihilists meant by nihilism are not the same, but they are not wholly distinct either. When we use the word "nihilism" today, we likely don't mean that we're worried people are trying to kill the Tsar. But we probably do mean that we're worried people are destructive, antisocial, and are at the very least willing to use violence to achieve their destructive antisocial goals. We might further expect that if someone were to be defending nihilism, it would be an angry teenager on Reddit, not a 70-year-old well-respected public figure on a stage at Harvard. And yet if someone like Wendell Phillips would give such a passionate justification of "Nihilism," then maybe we should rethink our preconceived notions about "nihilism," especially considering how many things are still named after this defender of the strange, wicked, and perverse.

"Doing Nothing"

Nihilism, not unlike time (according to Augustine) or porn (according to the U.S. Supreme Court), is one of those concepts that we are all pretty sure we know the meaning of unless someone asks us to define it. *Nihil* means "nothing." *-ism* means "ideology." Yet when we try to combine these terms, the combination seems to immediately refute itself, as the idea that nihilism is the "ideology of nothing" appears to be nonsensical. To say that this means that someone "believes in nothing" is not really much more helpful, as believing in something suggests there is something to be believed in, but if that *something* is *nothing*, then there is not something to be believed in, in which case believing in nothing is again a self-refuting idea.

Philosopher of nothing Jerry Seinfeld identified this problem when he made his first post-*Seinfeld* stand-up appearance on the *Late Show with David Letterman*. Seinfeld began,

The question is this: What have I been doing? Everybody says to me, "Hey, you don't do the show anymore, what do you do?" I'll tell you what I do: Nothing. Doing nothing is not as easy as it looks. You have to be careful. Because the idea of doing anything, which could easily lead to doing something, that would cut into your nothing, and that would force me to have to drop everything.[3]

Nothingness quickly becomes somethingness as soon as we try to talk about it. And yet, we talk about it all the time. "What have you been up to?" "Nothing." Exchanges like this are so common that it has become something of a reflex, as we frequently respond to such mundane questions with the answer, "Nothing."

But to most people such an answer would not be an example of nihilism. Nihilism is supposed to be something dark, something negative, something destructive. Saying you are doing nothing, however, is perfectly normal, as of course everyone knows that you are not literally *doing nothing*, which, as Seinfeld suggests, would be nearly impossible, but are simply indicating that you are *doing nothing worth mentioning*. Yet, if we do have these sorts of exchanges as frequently as I have suggested, then that would mean that we are frequently spending our time doing nothing worth mentioning. And if we are spending so much time doing nothing worth mentioning, then perhaps this exchange is closer to what we think nihilism means, perhaps this does indicate that our lives are not worth mentioning, that we are doing nothing with our lives, that we are nothing, that we *believe in nothing*.

To believe in nothing in this sense would then require not that we have a specific belief about nothingness that we could identify, but instead that we are living lives that accord with the belief that *life is nothing*. Nihilism as an "ideology of nothing" would mean not that we adhere to a discernible system of beliefs about nothingness, but rather that the beliefs we have, or think we have, are equivalent to nothing. For example, if we believe life is meaningful, and yet we spend our lives doing nothing worth mentioning, then our actions reveal that our belief about life is nothing worth mentioning, that it is worthless, that it is incapable of motivating us to do something rather than nothing.

It is here that we can begin to see why nihilism is typically viewed as something dark, negative, and destructive. For if we understand someone who is self-righteous—think of Holden Caulfield, Howard Beale, or Lisa Simpson—to be someone who would accuse others of nihilism, who accuses others of living nihilistically, then someone who is self-righteous is someone who believes that what others believe in is nothing. A self-righteous individual is therefore a critic, a skeptic, a heretic, someone who sees as nothing what others see as something, for which reason the self-righteous are often associated with smugness,

Nihilism as an "ideology of nothing" would mean not that we adhere to a discernible system of beliefs about nothingness, but rather that the beliefs we have, or think we have, are equivalent to nothing.

sanctimony, and superiority complexes. And it is this reduction to nothing of the beliefs of others that leads those others to see the self-righteous—the ones who not only do not share but actively reject the beliefs of others—as the ones who actually believe in nothing.

To be self-righteous is to see what is normal, what is accepted, what is popular, as nihilistic, as nothing, as meaningless. But to accuse others of being nihilistic is to be seen by those others as the one who is truly nihilistic, as the one who is truly a nihilist. This confusion about what it means to be a nihilist is important, as we will see, for example, when we get to Nietzsche, as he criticized what he saw as the nihilism all around him, and yet he described himself as a nihilist, leading people to criticize Nietzsche for advocating nihilism. These are distinctions that we will need to work out. There are the *nihilating* tendencies practiced by nihilists and there are the *nihilating* tendencies practiced by the self-righteous. Nihilism and self-righteousness are similar in that they are destructive, but they are opposed in the methods and purposes of their destructiveness.

Between the self-righteous and the rest of society there arises a war of beliefs. However, such wars are typically short-lived if they even take place at all. For as often happens in war, the side with the overwhelming numerical advantage simply wipes out the numerically disadvantaged side. This need not entail that the self-righteous are destroyed by society as more often than not they are simply ignored. Just imagine someone suddenly shouting in the middle of a mall about the absurdity of shopping in a mall. Though others would surely stop to see what is happening, it is far more likely that, rather than engage in a debate over the value of shopping or defend spending time and money in malls, the other mall goers would instead merely lose interest in the spectacle and return to their shopping unperturbed.

Yet the self-righteous, discovering that direct confrontation rarely leads to revolution, are likely to turn to whatever media are currently available in order to spread their critical, skeptical, heretical views. And it is for this reason that we can see why nihilism has become a topic of greater and greater concern as traditional media have been replaced by social media and shouting has been replaced by tweeting. Whereas previously the success of the self-righteous depended upon social, economic, and political conditions leading people to question the status quo, with the rise of radio, television, and, of course, the Internet, *questioning the status quo has become the status quo*.

Nowadays, to question the status quo, to rail against the system, to challenge the powers that be, is to be seen not as worthy of derision, but as worthy of acclaim, for if there is one thing on which political pundits agree, it is that whoever is popularly identified as the "change candidate" is the one who is most likely to win. At the same time, nihilists have become a mainstay of pop culture, as television shows like *Seinfeld* and *True Detective* and movies like *The Big Lebowski* have turned nihilists into icons and have turned meaninglessness into moneymaking machines. To be countercultural is now to be embraced by the culture.

At the same time that nihilists have become increasingly popular, so too does it seems that it has become increasingly commonplace to accuse others of being nihilistic. The charge of "Nihilism!" can now frequently be found not only in classrooms and on social media but also in op-eds and on cable news programs. Atheists are called nihilistic for not caring about faith. The religious are called nihilistic for not caring about facts. Conservatives are called nihilistic for not caring about social progress. Progressives are called nihilistic for not caring about social norms. Vegetarians are called nihilistic for not caring about farmworkers. Carnivores are called nihilistic for not caring about farm animals.

However, these trends would appear to be in conflict with each other, for how could being self-righteous become so popular at the same time that nihilism has become so pervasive? If the self-righteous are the enemies of nihilism, then why would a self-righteous culture put so many nihilists on TV? Or in the White House? Is this an indication of revolution or of hypocrisy? Is the current wave of self-righteousness really just an excuse to accuse others of nihilism without caring about what nihilism actually means? It is these questions that this book will seek to answer, for if we can learn to recognize the many varieties of nihilism, then we can learn to distinguish what is meaningful from what is meaningless, both with regard to others and with regard to ourselves. To begin, though, we must of course leave open the question of whether there exists anything that actually *is* meaningful—for if we are to start with a provisional definition of nihilism, it would certainly have something to do with taking meaningfulness for granted.

WHAT IS THE HISTORY
OF NIHILISM?

In this chapter I will provide a brief history of nihilism by providing a brief history of philosophers who revealed in their work some essential aspect of nihilism. The figures I will focus on did not (for the most part) identify their work as concerned with nihilism, but their arguments have helped to shape what has since come to be known as nihilism.

The word "nihilism" dates back to the eighteenth century and, in particular, to debates that took place among German philosophers over the implications of the metaphysics of the Enlightenment. However, the history of what nihilism represents can be traced back much further, for if a self-righteous individual is someone who tries to get others to realize that they believe in nothing and is in turn accused by others of believing in nothing, then Socrates was perhaps not only the "father of philosophy" but also the father of self-righteousness.

Socrates and the Cave

The Ancient Greek philosopher Socrates would walk around the Athenian marketplace, asking people to define concepts central to everyday life, concepts like love, honor, piety, knowledge, and justice. Once a fellow Athenian would give Socrates a definition, Socrates would test the definition, not only challenging Athenians to prove that what they believed to be true could actually withstand any and all attempts at refutation but also challenging Athenians to admit their beliefs to be false if Socrates's refutations were successful. In other words, Socrates went beyond merely trying to engage members of society in debate, as he was trying to force Athenians to question the beliefs their society was built upon, to question whether their society was based on the solid foundation of knowledge or on dubious foundations like custom and opinion.

The ultimate example of Socrates's foundation testing can be found in Plato's *Republic*, where Socrates goes from asking about the grounds of the concept of justice to burrowing down to what possibly lies beneath such grounds. In Book VII, Socrates asks his fellow Athenians to imagine prisoners who have been trapped in an underground cave since birth, given nothing to experience, nothing to learn, nothing to talk about, other than shadows. After describing the horrible lives of such prisoners, lives spent never knowing anything other than shadows, lives spent never knowing of the world beyond the cave, lives spent never knowing that they even are prisoners, Socrates declares, "They're like us."[1]

With this declaration Socrates makes clear that he is not merely asking his listeners to entertain a thought experiment, but is challenging his listeners (and, thanks to Plato, Socrates is also challenging us) to take seriously the possibility that everything they think they know about reality is an illusion. According to Socrates, we are like prisoners in an underground cave, not only because we accept as reality whatever we have grown accustomed to but also because, having grown accustomed to this reality, we would reject any challenge to this reality that was presented to us. Socrates wants us to realize not only that *seeing is believing* but also that *believing is rejecting* (or, as Sigmund Freud will later put it, *believing is rationalizing*). In other words, Socrates wants us to realize that we are nihilistic.

From the Socratic perspective, nihilism is a danger both epistemologically and existentially, for Socrates argues that the prisoners would not only continue to believe in shadows even if counterevidence was presented to them but would *kill* anyone who brought them this counterevidence, anyone who tried to convince them that their beliefs were false, anyone who tried to liberate them from their prison. The prisoners, not knowing that they are prisoners, would not see the cave as prison, but as home, just as the prisoners would not see the person who wants to take them out of the cave as a liberator, but as a madman. Whereas Socrates bases this argument on human nature, Plato further supports this argument with human history, as any reader of the *Republic* would know that Socrates had been put on trial and executed by the people he was trying to liberate for the crime of trying to liberate them.

From the Athenian perspective, Socrates was a heretic and a dangerous corruptor of the youth. Plato presents this perspective in his dialogues, as many of Socrates's interlocutors accuse Socrates of never putting forward his own beliefs and of instead merely trying to attack the beliefs of others. This view is indeed in keeping with the famous story of Socrates having been told by the Oracle of Delphi that he was the wisest man in Athens because he alone knew that he knew nothing. Whereas Socrates's interlocutors, such as Meno, liken Socrates to a torpedo fish, to a creature that numbs anyone who comes into contact with it, Socrates instead likens himself to a gadfly and to a midwife, suggesting that his purpose is not to confuse but to motivate and to help. Socrates therefore admits that his aim is to weaken people's certainty in their beliefs but argues that he does so in order to inspire them to replace their beliefs with knowledge. As Socrates says during his trial (in order to prevent them from trying to punish him by commanding him to stop questioning people's beliefs and thus to force them to instead punish him by execution), "The unexamined life is not worth living."[2]

Socrates thus helps us to recognize many of the characteristics that will later be used (centuries later once the word is invented) to identify an antinihilist. Socrates challenges people to defend their beliefs. Socrates erodes people's faith not only in what they believe to be true but in what they believe truth to be. Socrates withholds his own views and offers views that are radically inconsistent with views commonly held in society, leading others to accuse him of being a contrarian and of having no real views. Socrates tries to get people to embrace an alternate understanding of reality, and he is consequently accused of heresy and of attempting to corrupt society. Socrates inspires people to follow him, including people who will seek to violently overthrow society. Socrates inspires people to attack him, including people who will seek to execute him. Socrates inspires people to emulate him, including people who will seek to pursue his views to conclusions even more radical than those of Socrates.

Descartes and Dualism

Socrates led people to question the foundation of their beliefs, and he was executed for it. Plato, however, continued to spread Socrates's ideas, both through his dialogues and through creating an Academy to train others how to think and argue like Socrates. Plato's most famous student was Aristotle, who—as is depicted in Raphael's *The School of Athens*—ended up opposing Plato's views. Aristotle's critiques of Plato, and his conservative political views, helped to shift philosophy away from challenging people to question the foundations of everyday life to instead engaging in rigorous conceptual analysis. Aristotle's analyses helped to create new methods and fields of research, for which reason his name is on the first page of just about every college textbook. Aristotelian methods and ideas came to dominate intellectual research in Europe and remained dominant for centuries—that is, until Descartes came along.

The French soldier, mathematician, and philosopher René Descartes was educated in the Aristotelian tradition. But he was not satisfied with Aristotelian philosophy, in particular the marriage of Aristotelian philosophy and Christian theology known as Scholasticism. Descartes, like Socrates, was concerned that what was commonly claimed to be knowledge could not be accepted as knowledge unless we could be certain of the foundations of such claims. Yet whereas Socrates sought to test the foundations of knowledge through debate, Descartes instead preferred introspection, especially in the form of meditation.

Inspired by three dreams he had in a hot room on a wintry night on November 10, 1619, Descartes set out to revolutionize philosophy and science by reestablishing them on the foundation of certainty. Descartes carried out this revolution in several works, but it was his *Meditations on First Philosophy* (1641) that was his most famous and influential work. Descartes begins the *Meditations* by lamenting the number of falsehoods he had believed to be true in his life, and he argues that in order to avoid making such mistakes we must reject as false any beliefs that are held on the basis of uncertain foundations. Consequently, Descartes tests the certainty of every accepted foundation for knowledge and concludes that none can be trusted.

Our senses deceive us, so we cannot trust knowledge based on perception. We cannot distinguish dreams from waking life, so we cannot trust knowledge based on experience. Most famously, Descartes argues that unless we can somehow rule out the possibility of the existence of a malevolent God-like being—a being who could have convinced us that a false world is real, that nonexistent objects do exist, that $2 + 3 = 5$ when perhaps it doesn't—then we cannot trust knowledge, even mathematical knowledge, based on God's benevolence.

Yet what is most important for our purposes here is not what Descartes argues, but rather what he confesses. For after having come up with reasons to distrust the foundations of all possible knowledge claims, Descartes reveals that he nevertheless cannot maintain his distrust. Custom and habit have such a powerful effect on him that he finds that he cannot reject the knowledge claims he has believed in for so long no matter how untrustworthy he finds their foundations to be.

In other words, Descartes discovers that the most untrustworthy foundation of knowledge is not perception, experience, or faith, but himself. Or to be more precise, his nihilism. As Descartes concludes the First Meditation,

> I am like a prisoner who is enjoying an imaginary freedom while asleep; as he begins to suspect that he is asleep, he dreads being woken up, and goes along with the pleasant illusion as long as he can. In the same way, I happily slide back into my old opinions and dread being shaken out of them, for fear that my peaceful sleep may be followed by hard labour when I wake, and that I shall have to toil not in the light, but amid the inextricable darkness of the problems I have now raised.[3]

It is hard not to read this as Descartes returning to the cave from Plato's *Republic*, and imagining himself as one of the prisoners Socrates described. Yet whereas Socrates suggested that the prisoners would believe in the truth of what they see only because they do not know their predicament, Descartes suggests instead that the problem of belief goes even deeper. Descartes knows of his predicament, but knowledge of his situation is not enough to help him escape from it. Indeed Descartes admits that knowledge of his predicament only drives him to cling more desperately to the illusions he has found comfort in for so long, regardless of his knowledge *that they are illusions*.

Socrates said that the unexamined life is not worth living. Descartes has examined life and yet finds that the unexamined life was more "pleasant," more "peaceful," more *worth living*. The reason for this, as Descartes suggests, is that the examined life not only requires "toil" and "hard labour" but also may lead to "inextricable darkness" rather than to "the light" that Socrates promised would be waiting for anyone who left the cave. By raising the possibility of the existence of a malevolent God, Descartes brings skepticism to a new extreme, to an extreme that went beyond Socrates's cave. For Socrates, we are all in the cave together, and debating ideas with each other can lead us to the freedom of truth. But for Descartes, there is no *we*; there is only *himself*, only his doubts, only his uncertainties, because his thought that a malevolent God could exist has left him with nothing else.

Both Socrates and Descartes were antinihilists insofar as they both tried to inspire others to question and ultimately reject the foundations of their beliefs. But whereas Socrates was an antinihilist who accused others of nihilism, Descartes was an antinihilist who accused himself of nihilism. Descartes confesses that his rejection of the foundations of his beliefs is only temporary, for he cannot fight his urge to believe. Socrates presented the war between illusion and reality as a war between the unenlightened and the enlightened, but Descartes instead presents this war as a war within himself, as a war between his desire for happiness and his desire for knowledge.

Descartes, like Socrates, tries to combat nihilism by attacking its attachment to a world of illusions. Socrates did this by arguing that there is a better world beyond the world of experience, what he described as the world of the Forms, the world of truth, of understanding, of freedom from illusions. Descartes also fights nihilism with dualism, but unlike Socrates, Descartes describes a dualistic reality not outside of himself but within himself. For Descartes we embrace illusions because our reach exceeds our grasp, because our desire to know (the will) exceeds our power to know (the intellect).

Though his mind/body dualism is what gets the most attention, it is Descartes's will/intellect dualism that is far more important with regard to understanding nihilism. For Socrates, the key to combatting nihilism was to escape from the physical world into the intellectual world, and such escape was to be achieved either through debate or through death. For Descartes, the key to combatting nihilism is to escape from willful striving into scientific certainty, and such escape is to be achieved through both self-restraint and through rule following. If Socrates gave us the model of the antinihilist as a social reformer, then Descartes gives us the model of the antinihilist as a self-reformer.

Hume and Backgammon

Descartes revolutionized philosophy by trying to ground it in the power of the intellect. Though Descartes discovered that the intellect could destroy all faith in knowledge by coming up with an idea like the "Evil Demon," he also demonstrated that the intellect could replace faith with certainty, first by proving that he existed ("I think therefore I am") and then by proving that God existed. Or so he thought. For Descartes inspired a young Scottish philosopher named David Hume not only to carry out his own work of Cartesian skepticism—*A Treatise of Human Nature* (1738)—but to show that Descartes had not gone far enough with his skepticism.

According to Hume, Descartes's cosmological proof of the existence of God relied on a conceptual foundation that he had left unquestioned, the conceptual foundation of causality. Hume argues that if you really tried to build knowledge back up from the most basic elements of human nature (e.g., perception), then you could not claim that causality is something we can *know* to be true rather than something we can only *believe* to be true. Though we may see one event follow another, and see this sequence of events happen over and over again, it is impossible to see that this sequence of events *must* happen. In other words, we cannot experience necessity.

As Hume argues further, if we cannot experience necessity, then causality cannot be a basis for knowledge claims. For Hume, causality is a matter of probability ("The Sun will most likely rise tomorrow") rather than of certainty ("The Sun will definitely rise tomorrow"). So if we cannot know causality to be true, then we cannot have knowledge, as Descartes required, with regard to any claims made on the basis of causality (like Descartes's claim that God must exist because only an infinite being like God could have been the cause of his idea of an infinite being like God).

Having pushed Cartesian skepticism further than Descartes intended, Hume's empiricism destabilized the foundations of philosophy and science that Descartes had established on the basis of rationalism. Hume argues that much of what we believe to be true is so believed not because of the power of reason, but because of the power of experience. If we have a strong feeling about an idea, and we have a repeated experience of that feeling, then we can be led to elevate that idea to the rank of knowledge even though it has no greater certainty than an opinion.

Consequently, Hume likens philosophy to art, concluding that we must accept that our philosophical arguments are founded more on aesthetics than on rationality. As Hume writes,

Thus all probable reasoning is nothing but a species of sensation. 'Tis not solely in poetry and music, we must follow our taste and sentiment, but likewise in philosophy. When I am convinc'd of any principle, 'tis only an idea, which strikes more strongly upon me. When I give the preference to one set of arguments above another, I do nothing but decide from my feeling concerning the superiority of their influence.[4]

Hume here suggests that what we experience as discovering something to be true may in reality be the experience of discovering something to be preferable. We may think we are engaging in rational argument, but if our arguments are only agreed to or rejected based on "taste and sentiment," then we cannot distinguish facts from feelings, or progress from prejudice. In other words, supporting an idea may not be so different from supporting a sports team; we identify with a side, we take this identification to be meaningful rather than contingent upon factors beyond our control (like where we were born), and, most importantly, we want our side to win.

As Hume pursues the consequences of empiricism further and further, not only does he find that knowledge concerning causality unravels but so too does knowledge concerning himself. For Hume finds that his experiences are in a constant flux, a flux which does not suggest the existence of a stable "soul" or "self" or "mind," but which

We may think we are engaging in rational argument, but if our arguments are only agreed to or rejected based on "taste and sentiment," then we cannot distinguish facts from feelings, or progress from prejudice.

instead suggests that the flux is all there is, that he is nothing more than a "bundle of perceptions." Our memories create a narrative from out of these perceptions, a narrative based on the idea there must be a "self" who was the cause of this narrative, but having removed causality as a foundation for knowledge, it cannot function as a foundation for identity either. Descartes's skepticism led him to solipsism. But for Hume, it's doubtful whether his own "ipse" even exists.

Faced with such radical skepticism, with the idea that the self is a "fiction" our memories create for us, Hume concludes,

> I am confounded with all these questions, and begin
> to fancy myself in the most deplorable conditions
> imaginable, inviron'd with the deepest darkness,
> and utterly depriv'd of the use of every member and
> faculty.
>
> Most fortunately it happens, that since reason
> is incapable of dispelling these clouds, nature
> herself suffices to that purpose, and cures me of this
> philosophical melancholy and delirium, either by
> relaxing this bent of mind, or by some avocation, and
> lively impression of my senses, which obliterate all
> these chimeras. I dine, I play a game of back-gammon,
> I converse, and am merry with my friends; and
> when after three or four hours' amusement, I would

return to these speculations, they appear so cold, and strained, and ridiculous, that I cannot find in my heart to enter into them any farther.[5]

From a Socratic perspective, nihilism can be overcome by enlightenment. From a Cartesian perspective, nihilism can be overcome by self-restraint. But from a Humean perspective, nihilism cannot be overcome. It is simply a product of human psychology. Hume, finding himself in the cave, in the "deepest darkness," does not try to debate or reason his way out, but instead plays backgammon. Like Descartes, Hume discovers nihilism within himself. Unlike Descartes, he does not fight his nihilism, he embraces it. Nihilism is, as Descartes described, a comfort, a way to remain safe, a way to "obliterate all these chimeras," even if only by helping us to try to ignore them.

Kant and Crisis

Though Hume may have been happy to remain within the warm grip of his nihilism, he nevertheless helped to inspire others to abandon their nihilism. As the German philosopher Immanuel Kant famously said, it was Hume who awoke him from his "dogmatic slumber." Seeing that Hume had demolished the foundations of knowledge, leaving mere probability in its place, Kant was inspired to take up the challenge of resurrecting knowledge on new foundations. Kant achieved this task, not by showing that Hume was mistaken in the conclusions he drew from empiricism, but by arguing that Hume was mistaken in his methods, in trying to reconstruct knowledge by using empiricism. For Kant, we cannot begin from experience, as Hume tried to do, because experiences are not something we *have*, they are something we *create*.

According to Kant, Hume was doomed to end up lost in darkness and chimeras because causality simply does not operate in the way Hume imagined. Using the example of melting wax, Kant points out that though we cannot know what was necessarily the cause of the wax melting, we nevertheless know that *something* caused it. Kant thus criticizes Hume for having mistaken the inability to apply the law of causality with the inability to prove that the law of causality exists. Since causality and necessity are vital not only to knowledge but to how we experience the world, Kant suggests working backward, starting from what we do experience (e.g., the law of causality) and then trying to explain how experience must operate in order to have such experience.

Kant argues that Hume was correct that the necessity upon which causality depends cannot be found in experience, but this is because necessity is part of the conceptual apparatus our minds use in order to shape experience. In response to the skeptical question of how we can know that our subjective experiences of the world conform to the objective truth of the world, that what I see *as* red really *is* red, Kant makes the revolutionary claim that such conformity can be known because the world of experience is constructed by the mind. Space and time are not *out there*; they are *in us*—they are how we perceive reality. The *matter* of spatiotemporal objects that we receive through the mental faculty of sensation are *formed* in accordance with the mental faculty of the understanding. According to Kant, perception, and knowledge based on perception, are possible only because of the spontaneous activity of these faculties working together in harmony.

Kant's "Copernican revolution" thus rescues knowledge from Hume's arguments that we can never go beyond what we experience, and that what we take to be knowledge is in reality contingent upon what we have experienced up until that point. Kant instead creates the possibility for science to again be based on universal truths that are independent of experience (what Kant calls "*a priori*") rather than on merely contingent claims that are dependent on experience ("*a posteriori*"). We can have a priori knowledge because reason can discover universal truths—truths like every effect must have a cause—but the cost of such knowledge is having to accept the idea that experience is shaped by us rather than given to us.

Thanks to Kant, we don't have to worry about the empiricist problem of induction that Hume raised, the problem that claims based on past experience could be falsified by future experience, since experience is consistent in how it is (and always will be) shaped rather than in how it had (so far) been given. But this raises the idealist problem of invention, the problem that experience is *human* experience, or even just *my* experience, and that nonhuman experience, or non-me experience, may be completely different without our ever being able to know. If Hume's empiricism drove us to skepticism, then Kant's idealism could drive us to madness.

Kant's solution to this problem is to try to combine empiricism and idealism in what he calls "transcendental idealism." As Kant puts it, experience is *transcendentally ideal*, but it is also *empirically real*.[6] In other words, what we experience is based on our mental faculties but is based on our mental faculties operating in conjunction with reality. Kant distinguishes between things as they appear to us, and things-in-themselves, arguing that though we can only have knowledge about appearances, these appearances are nevertheless real rather than figments of our imagination.

Kant argues that reality exists both "phenomenally" (appearances) and "noumenally" (in itself), and that though we do not have access to the noumenal world, its existence is certain. Without an external world, we would have nothing to experience, not even ourselves, for which reason Kant refutes Cartesian idealism by showing that experience does not rest on the "I"; rather the "I" rests on experience. In other words there must be a noumenal world so that the phenomenal world can exist, since without the noumenal world the "I"—the "I" of Descartes, the "I" that exists only so long as it is thinking, which means only so long as there is *something to think about*—would not exist. If experience depends on my existence, and my existence depends on experience, then there must be something that exists that is both beyond me and beyond experience since otherwise we'd be trapped in a chicken-and-egg paradox.

It was Hume's nihilistic acceptance of skepticism that awoke Kant's quest to reestablish knowledge. Yet, in an ironic twist of fate, it was Kant's attempt to overcome such nihilism that actually led the philosopher Friedrich Jacobi to famously use the word "nihilism"[7] in a letter he published in 1799 to publicly repudiate the philosophy that Kant inspired. Similarly, in 1801, the novelist Heinrich von Kleist described, in letters to his fiancée, the crisis ("My sole, my highest goal has been destroyed, I no longer have one"[8]) that he experienced after reading Kant's philosophy. For both Jacobi and Kleist, to divide reality into the phenomenal and the noumenal, to divide things as they appear to us from things as they are in themselves, is to reduce life to nothing.

Jacobi and Kleist both read Kant as having essentially imprisoned us back in the cave of the *Republic*. Whereas

Socrates's prisoners did not know they were prisoners staring at shadows, Kant's prisoners do know they spend their lives staring at shadows, but they are expected to accept such seemingly meaningless lives since escape from the cave (knowledge of the noumenal) is impossible. In other words, Kant solved Hume's crisis, but his solution inspired a new crisis. Thanks to Kant, we can reestablish knowledge on the grounds of rational certainty, but at the expense of undermining our certainty in the meaningfulness of experience.

Hume may have left us with skepticism, yet it was a skepticism we could overcome by hanging out with our friends. But Kant leaves us instead with skepticism about our ability to even have friends, to know who our friends truly are, who our friends are *in themselves* rather than as they *appear to be*. Kant leaves us not even knowing who we truly are, who we are in ourselves as opposed to who we appear to ourselves to be. Kant made science meaningful, but he inspired a wealth of new questions about what makes life meaningful. Kant thus moves us away from what we could call *epistemological nihilism* (believing that knowledge is impossible) and instead moves us toward what we could call *existential nihilism* (believing that life has no meaning).

Yet we can find a response to the threat of existential nihilism in Kant's moral philosophy. Wanting to save morality from skepticism, from the skepticism produced by basing moral claims on contingent grounds like the existence of God or human experience, Kant argues that morality can be based instead on the certain grounds of rationality. Using the "purity" of reason, Kant discovers in rationality a "pure" moral law, a law which would hold for any rational being, in any situation, at any time. Actions are moral, according to Kant, if they can be universalized without creating a logical contradiction.

Kant provides a moral law free from the contingencies of human traditions and human experiences. Its truth, like the truth of the laws of science, is a priori. Yet, as Kant is forced to concede, humans are not perfectly rational beings, and thus the "impurities" of being human prevent us not only from being able to automatically obey the moral law but from being able to even prove that anyone has ever obeyed the moral law, including ourselves. An a priori moral law cannot, by definition, be proven in experience, just as the a priori law of causality could not be proven in experience. Hence, just as Kant preserved science from skepticism by removing its truth from experience, so too does Kant preserve morality from skepticism by removing its truth from experience.

Consequently, the meaningfulness of morality appears to have been removed by Kant just as he removed the meaningfulness from science. Kant reduces morality to a math problem, and like a math problem, Kant claims that we should not concern ourselves with whether it makes us happy, but with whether it is true. In fact Kant goes so far as to claim that we should obey the moral law even if it makes us miserable, even if it kills us, because, to the extent that we are rational beings, it is our "duty" to obey rational laws, and thereby, according to Kant, do we retain not our happiness, not our lives, but our "dignity." What is rational must be obeyed no matter the consequences, as consequences, like human experience, human happiness, and human traditions, are merely contingent, impure, phenomenal, and undignified.

Even "freedom" is obedience for Kant, as freedom is defined by "autonomy," which means that we are free only when we are obeying the laws ("-nomy") of the self ("auto-"). Oppression is thus defined by "heteronomy" or being forced to obey the laws of another ("hetero-"). But importantly the "self" that is to be obeyed is only the *rational* self, as obedience to desire, even to one's own desires, is for Kant to be heteronomous, not autonomous. As desires are not within our control (e.g., liking something is a discovery, not a choice), it doesn't make sense to Kant to associate desire with freedom, and thus Kant instead describes desire as heteronomous, as something *forced upon us*. For Kant, morality, dignity, and freedom can only be understood coherently if they are understood to be nothing other than obedience to reason. Consequently, the meaning of life is not to be found in happiness, but in duty, for, as Kant argues, it would make no sense that we are born with reason, with a faculty that is so often in conflict with our desires, if we were meant to be happy.

Just as Kant's answer to epistemological nihilism opened the door to existential nihilism, his answer to existential nihilism opened the door to what we could call *political nihilism* (believing that traditional human values are worthless because they are contrary to genuine human freedom). And indeed this form of nihilism became very popular in the wake of Kant's philosophy, as German, English, and Russian literature became filled with figures who were willing to reject anything seen as merely human in strict obedience to what was seen as a higher cause. Goethe's *Faust* (1808), Byron's *Manfred* (1817), and Turgenev's *Fathers and Sons* (1861) all featured protagonists who sought freedom in the form of overcoming human attachments, a freedom that they sought at any cost. In Russia, these figures existed not only in literature but also in the aforementioned political movement of self-identified "Nihilists" (1860–1881). These Nihilists sought to emancipate Russian society by destroying it, as they believed that only what could survive destruction was worth saving. And it was around this time that the most famous nihilist, Friedrich Nietzsche, similarly declared, "What does not destroy me, makes me stronger."[9]

Nietzsche and Diagnosis

Friedrich Wilhelm Nietzsche—the philosopher most associated with nihilism—was born in 1844 in Röcken, Germany. Nietzsche grew up in the shadow of both the Church of Lutheranism and the Church of Kantianism. Nietzsche's father was a Lutheran pastor who died when Nietzsche was five. At school he began to study classical languages, which ultimately led Nietzsche to pursue a career in philology. Though he was appointed as the Chair of Classical Philology at the University of Basel when he was only 25 years old, his ill health, and ill-received publications, kept Nietzsche from maintaining an academic career.

Nietzsche traveled throughout Europe for the rest of his life in search of a place where he could breathe more easily, both literally and metaphorically. However, Nietzsche's sister, Elisabeth Förster-Nietzsche, married a German nationalist and anti-Semite who tried unsuccessfully to start an Aryan colony in Paraguay called "Nueva Germania,"[10] and when it failed he killed himself. After Nietzsche fell ill (literally, he collapsed in Turin while trying to protect a horse from being beaten) in 1889, Elisabeth became the caretaker of both Nietzsche and his legacy. Thanks to her promotional efforts (and editorial distortions, which included forging letters and rewriting passages), Nietzsche is identified not only with nihilism but with Nazism. However, unlike his sister and brother-in-law, Nietzsche rejected German nationalism and opposed anti-Semitism, as he instead described himself as a "Good European."

Before Nietzsche fell ill, he was planning to write a book on nihilism. After she became his caretaker, Nietzsche's sister collected together his notes and published them after his death as *The Will to Power* (1901). These unpublished notes provide us with a vast variety of analyses of nihilism that Nietzsche had written in his notebooks over several years. For example, in Nietzsche's notes we can find such analyses and definitions of "nihilism" as the following:

> Nihilism stands at the door: whence comes this uncanniest of all guests? Point of departure: it is an error to consider "social distress" or "physiological degeneration" or, worse, corruption, as the *cause* of nihilism. Ours is the most decent and compassionate age. Distress, whether of the soul, body, or intellect, cannot of itself give birth to nihilism (i.e., the radical repudiation of value, meaning, and desirability). Such distress always permits a variety of interpretations. Rather: it is in one particular interpretation, the Christian-moral one, that nihilism is rooted.[11]

What does nihilism mean? *That the highest values devalue themselves*. The aim is lacking; "why?" finds no answer.[12]

Nihilism represents a pathological transitional stage (what is pathological is the tremendous generalization, the inference that there is no meaning at all): whether the productive forces are not yet strong enough, or whether decadence still hesitates and has not yet invented its remedies.[13]

Nihilism. It is ambiguous:
A. Nihilism as a sign of increased power of the spirit: as *active* nihilism.
B. Nihilism as decline and recession of the power of the spirit: as *passive* nihilism.[14]

The philosophical nihilist is convinced that all that happens is meaningless and in vain; and that there ought not to be anything meaningless and in vain. But whence this: there ought not to be? From where does one get *this* "meaning," *this* standard?—At bottom, the nihilist thinks that the sight of such a bleak, useless existence makes a philosopher feel *dissatisfied*, bleak, desperate. Such an insight goes against our finer sensibility as philosophers. It

amounts to the absurd valuation: to have any right
to be, the character of existence *would have to give the
philosopher pleasure*.[15]

However, as these notes were unpublished during his
lifetime, we have no way of knowing what Nietzsche's ultimate view of these notes was, whether he considered them
all to be part of his diagnosis of nihilism, or only some
of them, or maybe even none of them. Yet because these
notes were written while he was writing works he did pub-
lish, we can try to piece together his views on nihilism by
comparing his notes with his publications. I will here focus
primarily on his *On the Genealogy of Morals* (1887), as it
was his most systematic work, a work written at the same
time as many of his notes on nihilism, and a work that
he had hoped would help to spread ideas from his other
works to a larger audience.

In the preface to the *Genealogy*, Nietzsche writes that,
as a child, when he wondered about the origin of evil, he
reasoned that God, as "father" of all creation, must also
be the "*father* of evil."[16] But, due to a "peculiar scruple," a
scruple that he says put him at odds with his upbringing,
with his heritage, with his culture, with everything that
could be described as his "*a priori*," he learned to stop looking "*behind* the world" for answers to such questions. Using his philological training, Nietzsche instead looked at
the world itself and, in particular, looked at the languages

of the world. There he discovered that the further back he traced the language of morality—the language of "good" and "evil," the language that Kant took to be *pure*, to be *rational*, to be free of any empirical impurities like human history or human psychology—the more evidence he found that morality was not pure, but was the result of a struggle for survival.

Morality—or at least what the Europeans of Nietzsche's day took to be morality—was not absolute and universal as Kant believed but was rather the end result of a war between *rival moralities*. The discovery that "good" as a value had been applied by different cultures in different ages not only to different ways of life but to opposed, to contrary, ways of life revealed that there was no guarantee that what was accepted as "good" was *good*, nor that what was accepted as "morality" was *moral*. Having shown that Kant was wrong to have held that morality had a priori foundations, foundations whose truth would be independent of experience and thus independent of evolution, Nietzsche asked his readers to take seriously the idea that morality was not only a posteriori, was not only one morality among many possible conflicting moralities, but that morality was dangerous, that morality was *hostile to life*.

In the first essay of the *Genealogy*, Nietzsche uses his philological research to trace the etymological evolution of moral values back to its pre-Christian roots, back to a time when there were at least two competing value systems: "master" morality and "slave" morality. Before Nietzsche, Hegel had discussed the idea of ethical life arising from a struggle between equals, a struggle that resulted in the winner becoming "master" over the "slave," over the one who lost by being the first to flinch in their game of chicken. For Nietzsche, however, who is a master and who is a slave is determined not by struggle but by birth, by who is born strong and who is born weak. The strong rule simply because they can, for which reason they become stronger while the weak become instead smarter, as they are forced to outwit rather than outfight the masters. Thus, while the masters see themselves and their physical qualities as "good" and see those who do not share their qualities as "bad," the slaves instead see the masters and their activities as "evil" and see those who do not participate in such activities—that is, themselves—as "good."

Though Nietzsche is describing a time early in human history, it is not hard to see a similar pattern in our own early lives, as the masters are essentially *jocks* and the slaves are essentially *nerds*. Jocks take, while nerds plan. Jocks see themselves as good because they are strong and attractive, whereas nerds are weak, ugly, and therefore bad, fun to torment, but otherwise not worth thinking about. Nerds, on the other hand, hate the jocks, hate everything the jocks do, and define themselves as good by contrast, believing themselves to be capable of doing anything the jocks do, but to be *too good* to do such things.

Aside from the masters and slaves, Nietzsche identifies a third group, the "priests." The priests are those who were born as strong as the masters but who instead value cleanliness or "purity" above anything dirty or "impure." Thus on our Nietzschean playground, along with the jocks and the nerds, we also find the *preppy kids*, the rich kids, the kids who, like the nerds, see themselves as too good to participate in the activities of the jocks, but who, unlike the nerds, are not weaker than the jocks.

The fundamental question Nietzsche raises in the *Genealogy* is this: How did the slaves defeat the masters? According to Nietzsche, the values of the slaves, the values of humility, of abstinence, of self-denial and of self-sacrifice, are the values that won, the values that have become what we now accept as *moral*. We are the product of the victory of the slaves over the masters, a victory that was so decisive that we no longer even recognize that there was such a victory, that there was once competing value systems and competing moralities. It is for this reason that Nietzsche argues that we do not know who we are, as we take morality for granted, not recognizing the history and bloodshed behind it. Without knowing how the slaves defeated the masters—a defeat as improbable as nerds becoming more cool than jocks, or comic books and video games becoming more popular than sports—we cannot know who we are and why we value what we value.

Nietzsche's answer to the question of how slave morality won is that the slaves did not defeat the masters by destroying them, but by converting them. This conversion involved three elements: motive ("*ressentiment*"[17]), means ("instruments of culture"[18]), and opportunity ("Jesus of Nazareth"[19]). "*Ressentiment*" is Nietzsche's term for the psychology of the slaves, as the slaves did not merely resent the masters, but they hated the masters, they blamed the masters for their slavery, not only in the sense of their having been born into oppression but even in the sense of their having been born weak, vulnerable, and mortal. In other words, the slaves expected that if they defeated the masters, then they would finally become masters themselves. Consequently, as Nietzsche points out, early descriptions of Heaven by priests and even by saints made it clear that the reward of eternal bliss for having lived a "good" life was the knowledge that one's enemies, those who had lived an "evil" life, were receiving eternal torture in Hell. This perhaps helps to explain why religious art seems to be far more consumed with depictions of Hell than of Heaven.

Of course, telling someone who is oppressing you that he or she is going to go to Hell would likely not be enough to convince that person to stop. But with the arrival of Jesus, with the arrival of God in the flesh, the idea that Heaven and Hell actually exist was made far more real. As Blaise Pascal would later argue, the very possibility that Heaven and Hell are real should be sufficient for one to "wager" that it is safer to live *as if* they are real rather than risk finding out too late that you had bet wrong. More to the point, Jesus was portrayed as ushering in a new religion, a religion of love and redemption, a religion which would allow the masters to be forgiven for their "sinful" (warrior) lives and go to Heaven if they simply stopped being "sinners" (masters) and instead became "moral" (slaves). It was this portrayal which, according to Nietzsche, allowed the slaves to use Jesus as "bait" to convert the masters to the slave religion of Judaism by simply rebranding it as "Christianity."

With the conversion of the masters, it was possible for masters and slaves to live together and form a society. However, in order to achieve social stability, the former masters and the former slaves had to learn how to live in a society. This is how the priests rose to power. The priests taught the masters to live like slaves, to live in accordance with Judeo-Christian values, which led to the idea that being "moral" required learning how to repress one's instincts. In much the same way that schoolchildren are brought to museums in order to learn how to *look and not touch*, so too did the priests use what Nietzsche calls "the instruments of culture" in order to teach society how to *think and not act*. By convincing people that they had a soul, a soul which could be held accountable for their actions and which could be eternally rewarded or punished, the priests developed in humanity the ability to remember, to reason, to make promises, and, most importantly, to feel *guilty*. According to Nietzsche, memory, rationality, promise keeping, and guilt are not natural, but are rather the products of centuries of punishment and torture, not unlike how scientists use pain to condition lab animals to act rationally, to safely navigate the maze the scientists constructed for them.

And indeed, as Nietzsche argues, the priests created a world that was much safer for humanity than the world of masters and slaves. But this safety came at a high price. According to Nietzsche, repressing an instinct is not the same as removing that instinct, as instinctual urges cannot simply disappear but must instead be acted upon. Instinctual urges contrary to Judeo-Christian values— such as the urge to take pleasure in being cruel toward others—were repressed by being redirected, and since it was "immoral" to be cruel to others, members of society could only maintain their morality by redirecting their cruelty at themselves. This self-cruelty is what became known as "guilt," or what Nietzsche also describes as "the bad conscience,"[20] and it was by inventing guilt that the priests were able to maintain society. In other words, the moral society that the priests created was a safe society not because the morality they preached led people to stop being cruel, but because morality led people to associate being "good" with being cruel to oneself. And thanks to Jesus dying for our sins, this self-cruelty, this guilt, is inexhaustible, as our debt to God can never be repaid. Thus, for Nietzsche it is not an accident that the German word "Schuld" means both *guilt* and *debt*.

If self-cruelty is *good*, then self-denial and self-sacrifice are *the highest good*. These values, which we still today hold up as models of moral behavior, are what Nietzsche calls our "ascetic ideals."[21] The victory of Judeo-Christian values led to a society where instead of wanting to become masters, people should want to become monks. Not hurting others, not acting dangerously, not drinking, not smoking, not having sex, not being selfish, not being self-centered, and not being self-aggrandizing are all examples of monkish traits that are identified with the moral life. Yet, as Nietzsche points out, human nature is much more animalistic than monastic, for which reason trying to live a moral life requires that we try to live unnaturally, that we try to live lives that are *contrary to life*.

Nietzsche defines life as "the will to power,"[22] as life is for Nietzsche focused on change rather than stasis, on becoming rather than being, on improving oneself through struggle rather than stagnating for the sake of mere survival. The *will to power* is thus another way of saying the *will to will*, as seeking power has no purpose other than the ability to seek more power. Thus, to want to not grow, to

As Nietzsche points out, human nature is much more animalistic than monastic, for which reason trying to live a moral life requires that we try to live unnaturally, that we try to live lives that are *contrary to life*.

not change, to not improve, to want to remain who one is, is essentially to will to not will. Yet, according to Nietzsche, this willing to not will is precisely what the priests require of us in order to maintain social stability, in order to keep society safe, which we can now see means being safe from human instincts, safe from human nature, safe from human life. Judeo-Christian values and ascetic ideals aim at preserving society by championing self-cruelty, self-denial, and self-sacrifice. In other words, what we think of as "morality" was not *discovered* in pure reason by Kant but was *designed* to ensure that the meek shall inherit the Earth, an aim which just happens to be shared by both Christianity and by Kantianism.

The priests (a class which we can now see includes both Saint Paul and Saint Kant) created an ascetic society that has helped us to stay alive. But our survival has been achieved by encouraging us to avoid living. It is for this reason that Nietzsche argues that the priests replaced the danger of the masters with the disease of nihilism. Likening himself to a cultural physician, Nietzsche diagnoses this nihilistic sickness that he sees all around himself. This is the sickness that comes from living in a society that breeds mediocrity, in a society where humility is a virtue and pride is a sin, in a society that defines "progress" as learning to not act on one's instincts and to instead be civilized, to instead be *passive-aggressive*. If Nietzsche were alive today, he might see our "civilized society" as something like a giant bus, where everyone is motionless, praying for the ride to end quickly, sitting beside a bag strategically placed to avoid sitting next to anyone else, holding a smartphone to avoid looking at anyone else, and wearing earbuds to avoid hearing anyone else. In other words, we have come to see life as something to endure rather than enjoy and have come to see humanity as something to loathe rather than love.

Nietzsche sees the loss of the masters as the loss of not only a source of danger but also a source of pride. The masters represented what humans could achieve, and thus they provoked fear at the same time that they provoked admiration. With the conversion of the masters to Christianity, it was God who became this symbol of fear and admiration. But as Karl Marx similarly pointed out in his essay "Alienated Labor" (1844), the more powerful God became, the less powerful humanity became. Whereas the slaves wanted to be like human masters, Christians want to be like superhuman masters, asking no longer what humans can do, but instead, "What would Jesus do?" Living in the shadow of the masters forced the slaves to become clever enough to defeat the masters, but living in the shadow of an omnipotent supernatural being forced members of society to become repressed enough to be judged worthy of enjoying life after death.

The elevation of the supernatural and the reduction of the natural were for Nietzsche the primary causes of nihilism. The belief in a world beyond the world of experience, in a life after death, justified the asceticism preached by the priests, as self-cruelty, self-denial, and self-sacrifice were far easier to accept as ideals so long as one believed that the self that one tortured, denied, and sacrificed was not one's *true self*. And yet, though the priests taught that *this life* and *this world* were meaningless compared to the life and the world to come, in order to preserve society the priests also taught that suicide was a sin. In other words, whether one is a follower of Socrates or of Jesus, humans are to be understood as prisoners, forced to live meaningless lives in a meaningless world. The key difference though is that, with Christianity, we humans know who has imprisoned us, that our jailer is a good and perfect God, a God who created this prison even though its only purpose seems to be to test whether the prisoners can get released for good behavior.

As we have already seen, the more powerful God became, the more powerless humanity became. But it was also the case that the more powerful God became, the more contradictory the idea of God became. For why would God create such a prison? If God was good, then why torture his creations? And if God is all-knowing, why would God need to test his creations? It was because Christianity inspires such questions that Nietzsche associates nihilism both with the claim that "God is dead"[23] and with the claim that "the highest values devalue themselves."[24] To make God responsible for everything is to make humanity responsible for nothing, which is to make human existence meaningless, which is to make God's judgment of our existence meaningless, which is to make God's existence meaningless. The idea of God served to convert the masters and to create a civilized society, but the idea that God is all-powerful and all-knowing—an idea which was necessary to perpetuate the repression necessary to preserve society—could not ultimately sustain itself, as the repressed were eventually led to see God as nothing but the one to blame for their repression.

If the slaves hated the masters for their lowly existence, they had all the more reason to hate God, particularly as the destruction of the masters did not turn them into masters, but instead turned all of humanity into slaves. For this reason, according to Nietzsche, the priests strove to find methods to divert and to distract humanity from the growing dissatisfaction with the society the priests created. These methods aimed to again channel humanity's destructive impulses toward constructive activities, like destroying oneself rather than God or society. In the third essay of the *Genealogy*, Nietzsche describes five of these methods: self-hypnosis, mechanical activity, petty pleasures, herd formation, and orgies of feeling.[25]

Self-hypnosis is a way to avoid pain by putting oneself to sleep, such as by meditating, drinking, or watching YouTube. Mechanical activity is a way to avoid making

To make God responsible for everything is to make humanity responsible for nothing, which is to make human existence meaningless, which is to make God's judgment of our existence meaningless, which is to make God's existence meaningless.

decisions by following the orders of others, such as by obeying a boss, obeying a routine, or obeying a Fitbit. Petty pleasures are a way to avoid the feeling of powerlessness by making oneself feel powerful, such as by volunteering, donating, or swiping on Tinder. Herd formation is a way to avoid solitude by joining groups, such as by being on a team, being on a committee, or being on Facebook. Orgies of feeling—which Nietzsche singles out as "guilty" as opposed to the relative "innocence" of the previous four— are a way to avoid accountability by participating in a large outburst of emotions, such as by rioting, raving, or rage posting on Reddit.

It is the use of these methods that Nietzsche identifies as having prevented the destruction of society, but at the cost of having worsened our nihilism. Nietzsche thus likens the priests to bad doctors. The priests recognized that trying to be civilized beings living in a civilized society was making humanity sick. But rather than try to cure the sickness, the priests instead only tried to treat the symptoms and did so by merely prescribing more and more painkillers. These priestly medications thus helped to numb the sick, but this numbness only produced more nihilism, for numbness, like asceticism, is a rejection of life. To avoid pain, decision-making, powerlessness, solitude, and accountability is to avoid being human. To become numb therefore is only to become more sick, particularly as being surrounded by other numb humans is to be led to further loathe what has become of humanity. By making the sick sicker, the priests only made the nihilistic more nihilistic.

While priestly medications have made us sufficiently numb to remain in society, to remain bound to the values that society upholds, according to Nietzsche the result of this increasing nihilism is that society and society's values come to feel increasingly meaningless. God is still invoked, but "God" does not mean what it used to mean, much like when we say "God bless you" after someone sneezes, but as a reflex rather than as a meaningful act. Yet Nietzsche points out that though our nihilism "killed" God, we have not abandoned the role that God played in society. When God no longer fulfilled the role of the superhuman source of meaning in our lives, we did not try to give our lives meaning on our own, but instead merely sought out new superhuman sources of meaning. In this way we maintained our religious fervor even if that fervor did not remain attached to any particular religion.

Nietzsche thus argues that science is not the enemy of religion, but is instead a new religion, a new source of meaning, with its own priests, rituals, sacred texts, and life-guiding values and ideals. The priests of science (e.g., positivists) elevated scientific values like "objectivity" to superhuman heights, leading society to feel "enlightened," to feel that it had progressed beyond the "dark ages" of Christianity. "Good" and "Evil" may seem antiquated compared to the scientific values of "Objective" and "Subjective," but scientific values still serve the same purpose as religious values. Both sets of values have in common that they lead to an ascetic way of life, to a life of self-denial and self-sacrifice, to a life of repressing instincts whether because they are "sinful" or because they are "irrational."

That the death of God did not lead to the death of religion is what motivates Nietzsche's increasing focus on nihilism in his work. We can now see that though Nietzsche's diagnosis of nihilism was very complex and wide-ranging, Nietzsche's primary concern was with the idea of nihilism as the evasion of what it means to be human. Nietzsche identified such nihilistic evasiveness in Christianity, in Buddhism, in philosophy, in art, in science, and in culture. Nietzsche's diagnosis was that what these various versions of nihilistic evasiveness have in common is that they are a result of the repression required to live in civilized society, to live in peace rather than risk living in fear.

Nietzsche tried to get us to recognize how slave morality is self-destructive, how the morality of Judeo-Christian values and of ascetic ideals is hostile to life. But he was not advocating—contrary to what many of his followers and his critics believed—for the destruction of society and for the return to a life of fear, for the return to master morality. Nietzsche saw that replacing self-destruction with social destruction would do nothing to reduce our nihilism, as the death of God simply led us to seek out one new God after another. It is for this reason that Nietzsche's concern was less political than personal, as no political movement could solve our nihilism so long as we continued to reject life rather than embrace it.

After Nietzsche, nihilism became more and more seen as a topic worthy of philosophical exploration. Nietzsche had shown that while nihilism is destructive, its role in everyday life is to motivate activities that are commonly understood to be constructive, activities like meditating, exercising, volunteering, socializing, and partying. For this reason, Nietzsche inspired philosophers to investigate nihilism by investigating everyday life. Such investigations were aimed at revealing that nihilistic behavior is much more mundane than we realize, as popular culture came to be seen as a vehicle for promoting nihilism. Identifying nihilism thus came more and more to be viewed as not just an academic exercise but rather as part of a political struggle against the normalization of self-destructive practices, and against the demonization of anyone who would criticize what is *normal*.

WHAT IS (NOT) NIHILISM?

We can more carefully define what nihilism *is* by clarifying what nihilism *is not*. Having now traced the history of nihilism from Socrates to Nietzsche, we have seen that nihilism can be understood as a sort of umbrella term for a variety of related ideas. But once we begin to sort through these ideas it is easy to fall into the trap of thinking "Everything is nihilism!" which of course leads to thinking "Nothing is nihilism!" Thus in order to preserve nihilism as a meaningful concept, it is necessary to distinguish nihilism from concepts that are often associated with nihilism but are nevertheless different from nihilism, concepts such as pessimism, cynicism, and apathy.

Nihilism versus Pessimism

If optimism is hopefulness, then pessimism is hopelessness. To be a pessimist is to say, "What's the point?" Pessimism is often likened to a "Glass is half empty" way of seeing the world, but since it's only half empty this scenario might still be too hopeful for a pessimist. A better scenario might be that, if a pessimist fell in a well, and someone offered to rescue him, he'd likely respond, "Why bother? In the well, out of the well, we're all going to die anyway." In other words, pessimism is dark and depressing. But it is not nihilism.

In fact, from what we saw in the previous chapter, we might even go so far as to say that pessimism is the *opposite* of nihilism. Like nihilism, pessimism could be seen as arising from despair. The fact of our death, the frustration of our desires, the unintended consequences of our actions, the tweets of our political leaders, any or all of these could lead us to either nihilism or pessimism. However, where these two roads diverge is over the question of whether we dwell on our despair or hide from it.

To be with a pessimist is to know that you are with a pessimist. But you can be with a nihilist and have no idea. Indeed you could yourself be a nihilist and have no idea. Such a lack of awareness is the point of nihilism, as nihilism is all about hiding from despair rather than dwelling on it. This difference was illustrated by Woody Allen in

To be with a pessimist
is to know that you
are with a pessimist.
But you can be with
a nihilist and have no
idea. Indeed you could
yourself be a nihilist
and have no idea.

his movie *Annie Hall* (1977) when his alter ego Alvy Singer has the following exchange with a couple he stops on the street for advice:

ALVY   (*He moves up the sidewalk to a young trendy-looking couple, arms wrapped around each other*) You-you look like a really happy couple. Uh, uh … are you?

YOUNG WOMAN   Yeah.

ALVY   Yeah! So … h-h-how do you account for it?

YOUNG WOMAN   Uh, I'm very shallow and empty and I have no ideas and nothing interesting to say.

YOUNG MAN   And I'm exactly the same way.

ALVY   I see. Well, that's very interesting. So you've managed to work out something, huh?

YOUNG MAN   Right.[1]

Alvy Singer is a pessimist. The man and woman are nihilists.

What is most illuminating about this scene is that it shows how a pessimist can reveal the identity of a nihilist, just as it might be argued that the pessimism of the German philosopher Arthur Schopenhauer helped reveal to Nietzsche his own nihilism. Before they are confronted by Alvy, they are just a happily shallow and happily empty couple. However, when he asks them to explain their happiness, they are no longer shallow and empty; they are instead forced to awaken from their reverie and to become self-aware. It is not *that they are happy* that reveals their nihilism; rather it is their attempt to explain to a pessimist *why they are happy* that reveals their nihilism. On the surface, they are soul mates who have found each other. But surface is all that they are. The attempt to go any deeper reveals that there is nothing deeper. And it is precisely a pessimist who, when confronted with such a happy couple, would ask the "Why?" that reveals their nothingness.

If, as I suggested earlier, nihilism and pessimism are opposites, then nihilism is actually much closer to optimism. To see the glass as half full is to think that we should be happy with what we have rather than focusing on what is missing. But being happy with what we have can also be a way of remaining complacent, of ignoring what is missing so as to avoid having to seek change. Similarly, to believe that everything will work out in the end, that there is always light at the end of the tunnel, is to believe that life is teleological, that there is some goal or purpose— whether God or Justice—operating invisibly behind what we experience.

It is by believing in the existence of superhuman goals and superhuman purposes that we lose sight of human goals and human purposes. Likewise, when we elevate someone like Martin Luther King Jr. to the status of a saint or a prophet, we see him as more than a mere mortal, thus freeing ourselves from the responsibility of trying to emulate him since we simply have to be hopeful that someone like him will come again. If optimism leads us to be complacent, leads us to wait for something good to happen, or for someone else to make something good happen, then optimism leads us to do nothing. In other words, it is not pessimism but optimism that is similar to nihilism.

Nihilism versus Cynicism

In Ancient Greece, a Cynic was someone who lived like a dog (the Greek *kynikos* means "doglike"), or, to be more precise, was someone who lived by the Cynic philosophy of staying true to nature rather than conforming to what that person saw as social artifice. Today, a cynic is similarly someone who looks down on society and sees it as fake, though not because the cynic sees society as unnatural, but because the cynic sees the people who make up society as fake. To be cynical is to assume the worst of people, to think that morality is mere pretense, and to suppose that even when people seem to be helping others they are really only trying to help themselves. Believing in only self-interest, the cynic appears to others to believe in nothing. Consequently, cynicism can appear to be nihilism. But it is not nihilism.

Cynicism, like pessimism, is about negativity. However, whereas pessimism is about despair, about the feeling that life is pointless in the face of death, cynicism is instead much more about disdain than despair. A cynic wouldn't say that *life* is pointless but would just say that *what people claim about life* is pointless. A cynic can even enjoy life. In particular, a cynic can take pleasure in mocking those who claim that altruism exists, or that politicians are self-sacrificing public servants, and especially finds laughable the idea that we should try to see the good in people.

Pessimists are not nihilists because pessimists embrace rather than evade despair. Cynics are not nihilists because cynics embrace rather than evade mendacity. A key part of evading despair is the willingness to believe, to believe that people can be good, that goodness is rewarded, and that such rewards can exist even if we do not experience them. But to a cynic such a willingness to believe is a willingness to be naive, to be gullible, and to be manipulated. The cynic mocks such beliefs not because the cynic claims to know that such beliefs are necessarily false, but because the cynic is aware of the danger represented by people who claim to know that such beliefs are necessarily true.

A skeptic waits for evidence before passing judgment. A cynic, however, does not trust evidence because the cynic does not trust that anyone is capable of providing evidence objectively. The cynic would prefer to remain dubious than risk being duped, and thus the cynic sees those who do take such risks as dupes. For this reason the cynic is able to reveal the nihilism of others by challenging people to defend their lack of cynicism, much like how the pessimist reveals the nihilism of others by challenging people to defend their lack of pessimism.

Perhaps the best example of the revelatory abilities of a cynic is the argument between Thrasymachus and Socrates in the opening book of Plato's *Republic*. Thrasymachus is first introduced as mocking Socrates for questioning others about the definition of justice and then demands that he be paid in order to tell them what justice truly is. Once appeased, Thrasymachus defines justice as a trick invented by the strong in order to take advantage of the weak, as a way for the strong to seize power by manipulating society into believing that obedience is justice. Thrasymachus further argues that whenever possible people do what is unjust, except when they are too afraid of being caught and punished, and thus Thrasymachus concludes that injustice is better than justice.

When Socrates attempts to refute this definition by likening political leaders to doctors, to those who have power but use it to help others rather than to help themselves, Thrasymachus does not accept the refutation like the others do, but instead refutes Socrates's refutation. Thrasymachus accuses Socrates of being naive and argues that Socrates is like a sheep who thinks the shepherd who protects and feeds the sheep does so because the shepherd is *good* rather than realizing that the shepherd is *fattening them for the slaughter*. Socrates is never able to truly convince Thrasymachus that his definition of justice is wrong, and indeed Thrasymachus's cynicism is so compelling that Socrates spends the rest of the *Republic* trying to prove that justice is better than injustice by trying to refute the apparent success of unjust people by making metaphysical claims about the effects of injustice on the soul. Socrates is thus only able to counter cynicism in the visible world through faith in the existence of an invisible world, an invisible world that he argues is *more real* than the visible world. In other words, it is Thrasymachus's cynicism that forces Socrates to reveal his nihilism.

Here we can see that nihilism is actually much more closely related to idealism than to cynicism. The cynic presents himself or herself as a realist, as someone who cares about actions, not intentions, who focuses on what people do rather than on what people hope to achieve, who remembers the failed promises of the past in order to avoid being swept up in the not-yet-failed promises about the future. The idealist, however, rejects cynicism as hopelessly negative. By focusing on intentions, on hopes, and on the future, the idealist is able to provide a positive vision to oppose the negativity of the cynic. But in rejecting cynicism, does the idealist also reject reality?

The idealist, as we saw with Socrates, is not able to challenge the cynic's view of reality and instead is forced to construct an alternate reality, a reality of ideas. These ideas may form a coherent logical story about reality, but that in no way guarantees that the ideas are anything more than just a story. As the idealist focuses more and more on how reality *ought to be*, the idealist becomes less and less concerned with how reality *is*. The utopian views of the idealist may be more compelling than the dystopian views of the cynic, but dystopian views are at least focused on *this world*, whereas utopian views are, by definition, focused on a world that *does not exist*. It is for this reason that to use other-worldly idealism to refute this-worldly cynicism is to engage in nihilism.

Nihilism versus Apathy

Along with pessimism and cynicism, nihilism is also frequently associated with apathy. To be apathetic is to be without pathos, to be without feeling, to be without desire. While we are all occasionally given choices that do not particularly sway us one way or another ("Do you want to eat Italian or Chinese?"), such disinterestedness is what someone who is apathetic feels all the time. To be apathetic is thus to be seen as not caring about anything. The pessimist feels despair, the cynic feels disdain, but the apathetic individual feels nothing. In other words, apathy is seen as nihilism. But apathy is not nihilism.

Apathy can be an attitude ("I don't care about *that*") or a character trait ("I don't care about *anything*"). However, in either case the apathetic individual is expressing a personal feeling (or, to be more precise, *feelinglessness*) and is not making a claim about how everyone should feel (or, again, not feel). The apathetic individual understands perfectly well that other people feel differently insofar as they feel anything at all. And because the apathetic individual feels nothing, the apathetic individual does not feel any desire to convince others that they should similarly feel nothing. Others may care, but the apathetic individual does not, and because they do not care, the apathetic individual does not care that others care.

Yet apathy is still often seen as an affront, as an insult, as a rebuke by those who do care. For example, in MTV's *Daria* (1997–2002)—a show about a "highly apathetic"[2] high schooler—Daria Morgendorffer and her friend Jane Lane have the following conversation:

DARIA   Tragedy hits the school and everyone thinks of me. A popular guy died, and now I'm popular because I'm the misery chick. But I'm not miserable. I'm just not like them.

JANE   It really makes you think.

DARIA   Funny. Thanks a lot.

JANE   No! That's why they want to talk to you. When they say, "You're always unhappy, Daria," what they mean is, "You think, Daria. I can tell because you don't smile. Now this guy died and it makes me think and that hurts my little head and makes me stop smiling. So, tell me how you cope with thinking all the time, Daria, until I can get back to my normal vegetable state."

DARIA   Okay. So why have you been avoiding me?

JANE   Because I've been trying not to think.[3]

The apathetic individual can thus, like the pessimist and the cynic, reveal the nihilism of others, though, unlike the pessimist and the cynic, the apathetic individual does this without actually trying to. Whereas the pessimist and the cynic challenge others to explain their lack of either pessimism or cynicism, the apathetic individual is instead the one who is challenged, challenged by others to explain his or her lack of pathos. In trying to get the apathetic individual to care, the person who does care is forced to explain *why* he or she cares, an explanation which can reveal just how meaningful (or meaningless) is the reason the person has for caring.

The apathetic individual doesn't care. However, *not caring* is not the same thing as *caring about nothing*. The apathetic individual feels nothing. But the nihilist has feelings. It's just that what the nihilist has feelings for is itself *nothing*. And indeed it is because the nihilist is able to have such strong feelings, strong feelings for something that is nothing, that the nihilist is not and cannot be apathetic. Nihilists can have sympathy, empathy, and antipathy, but they cannot have apathy.

Nietzsche tried to demonstrate the feelings at work in nihilism in his argument against what he called the "morality of pity."[4] The morality of pity holds that it is good to feel pity for those who are in need, and it is especially good to be moved by such pity to help those who are in need. But, according to Nietzsche, what is often motivating the desire to help is how we are able to see ourselves thanks to how we see others in need, in particular how we see ourselves as capable of helping, as *powerful* enough to help.

The morality of pity is for Nietzsche not about helping others, but about elevating oneself by reducing others, by reducing others to their neediness, to a neediness that we do not have and that reveals how much we do have by contrast. Pity is nihilistic insofar as it allows us to evade reality, such as by allowing us to feel that we are better than we are, and that we are better than those in need. Consequently, we are able to avoid recognizing that we have perhaps only had better luck or have been more privileged.

The morality of pity drives us to feel pity and to feel good for feeling pity. Having such feelings is worse than feeling nothing, for if we feel good when we feel pity, then we are motivated only to help the individuals we feel pity for rather than to help end the systemic injustices that create such pitiful situations in the first place. Whereas apathy may help us to avoid being blinded by our emotions and to see situations of injustice more clearly, pity is instead more likely to motivate us to perpetuate injustice by perpetuating the conditions that allow us to help the needy, that allow us to see ourselves as *good* for helping those we see only as *needy*.

This is not to suggest, however, that we should try to achieve apathy, that we should try to will ourselves to feel nothing. Popular versions of Stoicism and of Buddhism advocate for calmness, for detachment, for trying to *not feel* what we feel. To force oneself to become apathetic is nihilistic, as to do so is to evade our feelings rather than to confront them. There is thus an important difference between *being* apathetic and *becoming* apathetic, between being indifferent because that is how one responds to the world and becoming indifferent because we want to be liberated from our feelings and attachments. Similarly, to become detached, not because of Stoicism or Buddhism, but because of hipsterism, is still to try to detach oneself from oneself, from life, from reality. So pursuing *irony* can be just as nihilistic as pursuing *apatheia* or *nirvana*.

WHAT IS NIHILISM?

In the previous chapter we saw that nihilism is about evading reality rather than confronting it, about believing in other worlds rather than accepting this one, and about trying to make ourselves feel powerful rather than admitting our own weaknesses. Nihilism is thus much closer to optimism, idealism, and sympathy than it is to pessimism, cynicism, and apathy. And yet we also saw that pessimism, cynicism, and apathy can help to generate nihilism as the negativity of such ways of life can lead people to seek out more positive ways of life. Such a conclusion suggests that a philosophy that argues that life has a meaning[1] is much more likely to be nihilistic than a philosophy that argues that life is meaningless.[2]

And yet for many people nihilism is simply the rejection of the meaningfulness of life. In his 1988 book *The Specter of the Absurd: Sources & Criticisms of Modern*

Nihilism, Donald Crosby offers a typology of nihilism that distinguished five different species of nihilism. Crosby writes,

> Common to the types of nihilism discussed in this chapter is an attitude of negation or denial, as is implied by the term nihilism itself. Each type denies some important aspect of human life. *Political nihilism* negates the political structures within which life is currently lived, as well as the social and cultural outlooks that inform these structures. It has little or no vision of constructive alternatives or of how to achieve them. *Moral nihilism* denies the sense of moral obligation, the objectivity of moral principles, or the moral viewpoint. *Epistemological nihilism* denies that there can be anything like truths or meanings not strictly confined within, or wholly relative to, a single individual, group, or conceptual scheme. *Cosmic nihilism* disavows intelligibility or value in nature, seeing it as indifferent or hostile to fundamental human concerns. *Existential nihilism* negates the meaning of life.[3]

As Crosby shows, even when we try to distinguish different types of nihilism, it is nearly impossible to avoid ultimately uniting them all into "existential nihilism" as "each type denies some important aspect of human life."

This helps to explain why nihilism is often associated not only with character traits like cynicism but also with philosophical positions like relativism. However, we must be careful here as treating different versions of nihilism as different versions of "an attitude of negation or denial" has the effect of reducing the significance of nihilism by making it seem like it is only an *individual* concern.

For this reason we need to come to a definitive understanding of what nihilism is. For example, is nihilism an attitude, a character trait, a philosophical position, or something else entirely? In order to achieve such an understanding, in this chapter I will explore four ways of thinking of nihilism. Each of these philosophical perspectives on the nature of nihilism can help to reveal not only what nihilism is but also why nihilism can be dangerous, and dangerous not just for individuals, but for the world.

Nihilism as Denial

As the contemporary analytic philosopher James Tartaglia announces in the title of his book—*Philosophy in a Meaningless Life: A System of Nihilism, Consciousness and Reality* (2016)—he believes that life is meaningless. Tartaglia defines nihilism as the denial that life is itself meaningful and so identifies himself as a nihilist. However, viewing nihilism as a statement of fact about reality, Tartaglia further argues that we are wrong to think of nihilism as bad or as negative or as in any way motivating bad or negative actions. Comparing life to a game of chess, Tartaglia suggests that the moves of the game are meaningful even if the game is itself meaningless, and so similarly we can find meaning in our lives even if life is *itself* meaningless. Indeed Tartaglia sees that we already do find meaning in our lives every day without having any evidence or reason to believe that life is itself meaningful, and so we should not assume that the meaninglessness of life is somehow some sort of existential or moral disaster.

Nihilism is for Tartaglia descriptive rather than prescriptive. While we are absorbed in the world, in the "frameworks" of our everyday lives, we are, according to Tartaglia, driven to act in certain biological and social ways, in ways that we find meaningful. We then analogize from the meaning of parts of life to the meaning of the whole of life itself, assuming that if our actions have a point, then the point of our actions must have a point as well. However, following Heidegger, Tartaglia sees in our experiences of anxiety and boredom an "attunement" to nihilism, an ability to free ourselves from our everyday frameworks and to gain sight of the pointlessness, the sheer contingency, of these frameworks. Yet Tartaglia sees our ability to move from anxiety and boredom back to absorption in these frameworks as proof that—contrary to Nietzsche—nihilism has no practical or motivational power. Tartaglia is thus critical of Nietzsche for having seen nihilism as something *dangerous* and as something to be *overcome*, rather than recognizing it as simply a *fact* and a fact that we can and do easily *ignore*.

Tartaglia's deflationary approach to nihilism leads him to see every other philosopher who has focused on nihilism as having had an overinflated sense of nihilism's importance. For Tartaglia it is something of a category mistake to think that the question of the meaning of life is itself meaningful in our day-to-day lives. The question of whether life is itself meaningful is for Tartaglia a metaphysical question, and so philosophers who think nihilism is negative or dangerous mistakenly believe that metaphysics matters as much in the daily lives of regular people as it does to philosophers.

Boredom and anxiety may reveal to us the meaninglessness of our activities, but since people—people who are not philosophers—are able to stop being bored or anxious and continue on with their lives, Tartaglia concludes that the truth of nihilism can be revealed to us without it making us suicidal or immoral. If people do become suicidal or immoral after discovering the truth of nihilism, that is not, for Tartaglia, the fault of nihilism, but of the illusion such people were previously laboring under. If we had been living our lives and trying to be good while nihilism was nevertheless true, then, according to Tartaglia, nothing more should be changed by discovering the truth of nihilism than having a mistaken metaphysical belief replaced with a true metaphysical belief.

Tartaglia thinks that if people try to be good, become bored, find life to be meaningless, stop being bored, and go back to trying to be good, then it is a mistake—a mistake made by Nietzsche and everyone who followed him—to think nihilism has any power over us. Tartaglia writes,

> I think that Nietzsche and many other philosophers have massively overestimated the motivational and moral significance of belief in overall purpose. Such belief is not essential to framework engagement, after all; if it were, then it is doubtful we would have ever heard of nihilism, since nobody would have been motivated enough to write about it. Perhaps such belief is very important to some religious people's framework engagement, especially in the moral sphere. But it cannot always be essential, because people do sometimes lose their faith and carry on.[4]

Tartaglia claims that if people can lose faith and yet continue on as before, then faith must not have been as "essential" as people—or philosophers like Nietzsche— have assumed.

However, this criticism of "Nietzsche and many other philosophers" is based on a misunderstanding of what Nietzsche and these many other philosophers were focused on in their analyses of nihilism, for it was precisely our ability to "carry on" that concerned Nietzsche and those who followed in his wake. Such philosophers did not think that nihilism was a statement of fact about reality, something about which one made truth claims. Rather nihilism was seen as a reaction to reality. Discovering life is meaningless is not nihilism for Nietzsche; rather discovering life is meaningless *and yet going on with our lives anyway* is nihilism. What Tartaglia views as the way to respond to nihilism—to stop being bored or anxious and just reimmerse ourselves in our daily lives—is precisely what Nietzsche meant by nihilism. In other words, what Nietzsche wants us to overcome is not what Tartaglia means by "nihilism" but rather what Tartaglia means by "life."

Tartaglia treats nihilism like the solution to a math problem. If you think math is meaningful, that pi is somehow significant in a cosmic sense, then you have a problem, a problem that can be solved by nihilism. Nihilism would then not affect the truth of math, but would only reveal the lack of truth about whatever metaphysical implications we have mistakenly derived from math. And since metaphysical implications are not what most people are worried about during most of their lives, nihilism is not something most people are worried about during most of their lives.

However for Nietzsche, as we have already seen, nihilism is about what's in the world, not what's behind it.

According to Nietzsche, the meaninglessness of life is due not to the nature of the universe, but to the nature of our culture. Life *is* meaningful, but only if *we live*. But to live meaningfully—to live as humans, to live in accordance with our own values rather than those that have been imposed on us—would endanger our culture and would endanger those who are powerful because of our culture. So to protect our society, those in power have led us to believe that there is only one way to be moral, that to be moral is to achieve self-control. We learn to control our urges, our desires, our instincts, and go about our daily lives as civilized adults. We do this, though, not because we *want* to live such lives, but because we have been raised to believe that we *should want* such lives. Trying to live the lives that we *should want* is, according to Nietzsche, what makes us nihilistic, for which reason we come to see death as freedom, as freedom from life, from what our culture has defined as life, from what Tartaglia has defined as life.

Tartaglia sees that our lives are meaningless, but he simply accepts this as a fact of reality. This acceptance leads Tartaglia to advocate that we try not to think about it, that we go back to living our meaningless lives. Tartaglia writes,

> As to the question of what we should do upon realizing the truth of nihilism, then, there may be more than a little relevance in Lin-Chi's advice to

"Just act ordinary, without trying to do anything in particular. Move your bowels, piss, get dressed, eat your rice, and if you get tired, then lie down."[5]

What Tartaglia accepts as the way to live our lives is what Nietzsche would see as nihilism in the most meaningful sense of the word. Tartaglia may appear to be in agreement with Nietzsche about the idea that nihilism is about living in denial, but what Nietzsche means by "denial" is what Tartaglia means by "acceptance." Tartaglia's treatment of nihilism as an unimportant concern thus results in the treatment of life as an unimportant concern.

Nihilism as the Denial of Death

For a deeper understanding of what nihilism means, we must then seek out a deeper understanding of what life means, such as can be found in the philosophy of existentialism. Existentialism can be traced back to the work of the Danish philosopher Søren Kierkegaard. Even just the titles of his works—such as *Fear and Trembling* (1843), *The Concept of Anxiety* (1844), and *The Sickness unto Death* (1849)—evoke the angst-ridden themes that are associated with existentialism, themes such as mortality, faith, and hypocrisy. The German philosopher Martin Heidegger is also an important foundational figure for existentialism.

Though Heidegger was a critic of existentialism, his work was nevertheless influential to existentialists. Particularly influential was his *Being and Time* (1927), in which he explores the "inauthenticity" of everyday life insofar as it is occupied with pointless activities like chitchat that help us to avoid the anxiety of confronting death that would make us "authentically" human.

However, existentialism is most often associated with French philosophers, with smoking, with drinking wine, and with being obsessed with death. None of this is wrong, but it does tend to focus our attention more on *who* the existentialists were rather than on *what* they were writing about. And indeed that existentialism has come to be associated more with their biographies than with their books is precisely the sort of superficiality that Jean-Paul Sartre, Simone de Beauvoir, and Albert Camus were trying to reveal in both their philosophical and their literary writing.

What Sartre, de Beauvoir, and Camus have in common in their work, and in common with Kierkegaard and Heidegger, is a concern with the question of the meaning of life. As we have already seen, this question has been a perennial concern for philosophers and, in particular, a metaphysical concern. What was different in how existentialists approached this question was how the experience of living through World War II made life seem to be not only meaningless but *absurd*.

Millions of people were being killed. Nazism and Fascism were spreading. The end of the world appeared to be imminent. And yet people continued to eat, to work, to gossip, to buy groceries, to sleep, to go on living as if nothing had changed. To see the routines that make up normal life continue when life was decidedly abnormal was to see how such routines not only help to make life easy to navigate but also help to make life easy to ignore. Whether faced with global war or with our own mortality, by maintaining order, regularity, and discipline we are able to reduce ourselves and the world to the most mundane concerns and so avoid having to think about anything more than what we're going to eat for dinner. In other words, we live lives that are absurd.

Yet, as existentialists argue, we paradoxically achieve this reduction through transcendence. We act as if life doesn't matter, but we do this because we believe that death doesn't matter. Seeing ourselves as beings who were created, we see ourselves as like other created things, and thus we see ourselves as having a creator, a creator that imbued us with an essence, an essence that transcends our individual existence. Whether we see this creator as God or as DNA is less important than we tend to assume, as in both cases we see ourselves as having been created with an essence, an essence that defines us as human and that gives us a purpose as part of humanity. What we do in our everyday lives can thus be seen from this perspective

Whether faced with global war or with our own mortality, by maintaining order, regularity, and discipline we are able to reduce ourselves and the world to the most mundane concerns and so avoid having to think about anything more than what we're going to eat for dinner.

as the result not of our individual freedom, but of our essence, or, as we more commonly call it, our *human nature*.

For denying the existence of God and for denying that life has a purpose, the existentialists were seen as nihilistic atheists. But the existentialists were not trying to advocate for atheism, for as we have already seen, DNA can serve the same explanatory function as God. Rather, the existentialists were trying to reveal that it is our belief in human nature that is nihilistic. When we justify our actions by saying that we're "just being human"—whether we think humans were created by God or programmed by DNA—we're avoiding having to take responsibility for our actions. Relying on human nature to explain our actions is to see ourselves as determined rather than as free, to see ourselves as things that can be determined rather than as humans who can make decisions for ourselves.

Sartre states that the motto of existentialism is that "existence precedes essence."[6] In other words, *that we are* comes before *what we are*. If we have an essence, then it comes from our decisions, not from any supernatural creator or genetic inheritance. We are not made; we are instead what we make of ourselves. For this reason we can only have the freedom that we at least claim to want if we recognize that freedom and responsibility are two sides of the same coin. Following Heidegger, existentialists see our denial of responsibility and of freedom as the result of our denial of death.

To recognize that we could die at any moment would require that we take every moment of our lives seriously, as seriously as if it were our last. But because we do not want such responsibility, we act as if we're going to live forever, and we see such a way of life as free. We may say that we know we're going to die, but we view death as something that would happen far in the future or that science and technology might somehow cure. Consequently, we do not take our daily lives seriously and do not take our decisions seriously, and thus the only freedom we exercise is the freedom to blame others, to blame God, or DNA, or society, or anyone but ourselves, for who we have become and how our lives have turned out.

This is not to say, however, that others do not play a role in how we turn out. Rather, existentialists want us to recognize our willingness to accept the illusion that what is contingent (e.g., character) is actually necessary and that what is necessary (e.g., death) is actually contingent. As de Beauvoir argues in *The Second Sex* (1949), "One is not born, but rather becomes, woman."[7] We are willing to accept the idea that women are different from men due to differences in chromosomes because such ideas relieve the pressure of having to define ourselves by our actions rather than by our genetics. Moreover, we do not question the source of distinctions like "women" and "men" but instead embrace such distinctions and try to live in accordance with them, letting them define who we are and determine who we should be.

Women should always be women. Men should always be men. Heroes should always be good. Villains should always be evil. Such narratives are comforting. They replace the absurdity of existence with the clarity of essentialism. Yet they are comforting precisely because they are fictions, fictions that we are born into and that we perpetuate, fictions that transform the anxiety-inducing gray of life into the reassuring black-and-white of a 1950s sitcom. Black-and-white labels make life easier, but they do so by making life lifeless.

Existentialism reveals that in trying to avoid responsibility, we end up avoiding freedom, and that in trying to avoid death, we end up avoiding life. Nihilism is thus seen as the result of our fear of death, and so the more we flee from death, the more nihilistic we become. To say that life is meaningless, as the existentialists do, is not to advocate nihilism but to combat it. By removing the false sources of meaning we rely on (such as God or DNA), we can confront the fact that we are alone and embrace the consequence of that fact: that we alone are capable of giving meaning to our lives.

Nihilism as the Denial of the Death of Meaning

Existentialism was so associated with the lives of Sartre, de Beauvoir, and Camus that their deaths could not help but bring about the decline of existentialism. Postmodernism, however, is not associated with any particular figure or figures. Indeed "postmodernism" has become such a term of abuse or of mockery that few, if any, individuals want to be associated with it, let alone identify themselves as postmodern. Therefore, there might not be any agreement about what "postmodern" means other than as a term to describe that which we don't understand, that which seems incapable of being understood, and that which appears to have been made in order to challenge our beliefs about our being able to understand anything. In other words, postmodernism is seen by many as not only nihilistic but as purposefully nihilistic, as nihilism made hip, as *performative nihilism*.

One of the few exceptions to the rule that no one wants to be identified with postmodernism is the French philosopher Jean-François Lyotard, who in 1979 published *The Postmodern Condition: A Report on Knowledge*. Invoking the concept of "language games" from the *Philosophical Investigations* of Ludwig Wittgenstein, Lyotard argues that every field of knowledge, every academic discipline, every science, operates through specific narratives with their own gamelike rules in order not only to transmit knowledge but even to legitimate its claims as knowledge. Claims are written, presented, published, interrogated, and challenged all in accordance with these rules, rules which are not written down and formalized, but which all participants in each field of knowledge come to learn and to perpetuate. What makes these language games more than *just games* is that their legitimation practices are themselves legitimated by narratives that exist outside each field of knowledge, by narratives that are accepted by society as a whole as providing a foundation for the field of knowledge, by narratives that Lyotard calls "metanarratives."[8]

Or at least that's how knowledge operated before the postmodern era. According to Lyotard, with the rise of computer technology, metanarratives have lost more and more of their legitimating power as knowledge has increasingly come to be seen as *information*. Metanarratives about scientists working for the good of humanity and seeking knowledge for its own sake have become outdated. To see knowledge as information is to see knowledge as power, as that which must have not only explanatory power within the field of knowledge but also political and economic power within society. The claims of scientists were never legitimated solely by scientists, as government funding and public support have always been important aspects of legitimation. Yet more and more governments fund and publics support only that which is *productive*, only that which produces the information necessary to make political and economic decisions. In other words, what is *true* has become less important than what is *profitable*. Consequently, the humanities have less funding and less support today than do the STEM fields of science, technology, engineering, and mathematics, the fields that produce what is more easily recognizable as truth as they produce what is more easily measured in profits.

Yet the bifurcation of humanities and STEM has eroded the legitimacy of both. Humanities produced the metanarratives that legitimated scientific knowledge, whether these metanarratives were spiritual or moral, as they embedded scientific pursuits into the pursuit of the meaning of life. At the same time, because scientists engaged in language games like those of the humanities, they helped to legitimate the language games of the humanities. But when scientists no longer needed to explain their activities and only needed to produce results, the language games of spirituality and of morality were replaced by the language games of output and of profit. Scientific and technological progress is, however, still identified with *human progress*, but with the decline of the humanities the metanarrative of "human progress" cannot speak to us in any other language than that of cost-benefit analysis.

Lyotard writes, "Simplifying to the extreme, I define *postmodern* as incredulity toward meta-narratives."[9] Postmodernism is the recognition that the narratives, the ideas, and the values we use to give life meaning are empty shells—or, to be more precise, the recognition that these narratives, ideas, and values have *always been* empty shells. The rise of computer technology did not undermine the

Postmodernism is the recognition that the narratives, the ideas, and the values we use to give life meaning are empty shells—or, to be more precise, the recognition that these narratives, ideas, and values have *always been* empty shells.

fabric of society; instead it revealed it, and what was revealed was that beneath the fabric there was *nothing*. What Lyotard sees as the crisis of legitimacy is not that the legitimation practices of the sciences have become corrupted by capitalism, but that—thanks to capitalism—we have become aware of the fact that the legitimation of the sciences was produced by practices, by nothing but practices, by practices that were themselves legitimated by nothing other than practices.

Postmodernism, however, does not lament the crisis of legitimacy, but welcomes it. To recognize that meaning is a production, a production of human practices, is to recognize the creative possibilities that surround meaning and to be free of the stultifying illusion that meaning is eternal, universal, and immutable. Rather than accept traditional narratives, ideas, and values as the bedrock of reality, postmodernism contends that reality has no bedrock, no foundation, other than practices, practices such as those surrounding the acceptance of such foundations as *discovered* rather than as *invented*.

The antifoundationalism of postmodernism, the idea that meaning is constructed rather than concrete, has been seen by critics as tantamount to promoting relativism, solipsism, and anarchy. To argue that there is no foundation for what we find meaningful and that we can consequently redefine the meaning of what is meaningful is to be seen as arguing that meaning is meaningless. For if something can mean anything, then everything means nothing. Critics thus see postmodernism as nihilistic.

Yet, from the perspective of postmodernism, such critics are merely clinging to meaning as given rather than interrogating the givenness of meaning. To reify human creations and treat them as though they were discoveries, as though they were found by us rather than made by us, is not only to deny human agency but also to reject the meaning of meaning. It is thus the critics of postmodernism, the foundationalists, who embrace meaninglessness by not admitting the need to investigate the nature and history of meaning.

What these critics misunderstand is that postmodernism is not advocating for the social construction of meaning but is rather arguing that meaning is and always has been socially constructed. To deny social construction is thus to deny reality. Foundationalists assume that there must be some ultimate ground to meaning—such as God or nature or scientific facts—and that postmodernism is a rejection of such grounds in the name of revolution. But postmodernists argue instead that there is nothing to reject, that there is nothing against which to revolt, because there is no ultimate ground to meaning. Postmodernism is thus not opposed to foundations, but to foundationalism, for while foundations have complicated cultural and political histories that need to be investigated, foundationalism is the rejection of such investigations due to the

To deny social construction is thus to deny reality.

unwillingness to see that "God" and "nature" and "scientific facts" have histories behind them.

Postmodernism can thus be seen as having taken the insight of existentialism that "existence precedes essence" and having applied it not just to humanity but to everything. Yet, because Sartre coined this existentialist motto in order to make clear why humans are not like anything else and why humans can therefore not be defined in the way that objects are, there appears to be a tension between existentialism and postmodernism.

For existentialism, nihilism arises due to a rejection of the meaning of death, which leads to a rejection of the meaning of freedom, of responsibility, and, consequently, a rejection of the humanity of humanity. For postmodernism, nihilism arises due to a rejection of the death of meaning, which leads to a rejection of history, of language, of creativity, and, consequently, a rejection of the meaning of meaning. But then postmodernism would appear to see existentialism as nihilistic for having constructed a foundationalism centered on death having an eternal and immutable meaning. And likewise existentialism would appear to see postmodernism as nihilistic insofar as the antifoundational claim that all meaning is socially constructed and mutable could be seen as an evasion of death by denying that death has any inherent meaning.

While existentialism and postmodernism may oppose each other over the meaning of death, what should concern us here is that they nevertheless appear to agree on the meaning of nihilism. Whereas existentialism sees nihilism as resulting from the denial of death, postmodernism sees nihilism as resulting from the denial of the death of meaning. In both cases, though, nihilism is understood to be an evasion of reality, whether by not being willing to face what it means to be human or by not being willing to face the humanity of meaning. More specifically, both for existentialism and for postmodernism, nihilism is an evasion of reality in the form of an evasion of freedom.

Nihilism as the Denial of the Death of the Meaning of Childhood

Simone de Beauvoir—an existentialist who was far more postmodern than either Sartre or Camus—provides a portrait of the nature of nihilism in her 1948 work *The Ethics of Ambiguity*. Inspired by Descartes's claim that adults are unhappy due to having previously been children, de Beauvoir describes how nihilism is related to the attempt to become a kid again. Children find themselves in a world not of their own making, in a world where everything has already been figured out by adults, in a world of definitions to learn and rules to obey. De Beauvoir labels the world of adults as seen by the child as the "serious" world in order to distinguish it from the world of frivolity that the child feels free to experience since—thanks to adult seriousness—nothing the child does seems to matter.

As we grow up, however, we lose our childish innocence and discover that our view of the world was naive, that the world has not been figured out, that our lives are not as predetermined as they appeared to be, and that our actions are far more consequential than we realized. Childhood thus proves to have been not a freedom from responsibility but a freedom from reality, a freedom from *the reality of freedom*. The loss of such freedom, according to de Beauvoir, can drive us to go beyond becoming nostalgic for our childhood and to try to make ourselves children again by seeing the world as we did when we were children. De Beauvoir calls this the "spirit of seriousness,"[10] for individuals consumed by such nostalgia try to make real the serious world of their childhood imagination.

Serious people evade freedom and responsibility through seeking infantilism and paternalism. Serious people turn themselves into children, wanting nothing more than definitions to learn and rules to obey. They thus require some external authority that can provide such definitions and such rules and that can guarantee that these definitions and rules will remain unchanging and absolute. Hence, serious people say things like "I know my rights!" in much the same way that children say "My daddy said don't do that!" for in both cases there is an appeal to an external authority whose mere existence is seen as sufficient to require that everyone *must* behave in accordance with the dictates of that authority.

But just as fathers can say that everything will be all right and yet children still experience pain and tragedy, so too can rights claim to protect us and yet violations can occur without penalty. Children and serious people are thus both ultimately forced to realize that no external authority can serve as the guarantor that they required, the guarantor that life will turn out as promised, that justice will be served, that the good guys will win, and that the pain and suffering we experience will ultimately prove to have had a purpose. In other words, no external authority can prevent either children or serious people from having to confront the ambiguity, the volatility, and the inexplicability of life.

According to de Beauvoir, just as children—for whom life did not turn out how they imagined it to be—can grow up to become serious people, so serious people—for whom life did not turn out how they desired it to be—can further regress and become nihilists. De Beauvoir writes,

> This failure of the serious sometimes brings about a radical disorder. Conscious of being unable to be anything, man then decides to be nothing. We shall call this attitude nihilistic. The nihilist is close to the spirit of seriousness, for instead of realizing his negativity as a living movement, he conceives

his annihilation in a substantial way. He wants to *be* nothing, and this nothing that he dreams of is still another sort of being, the exact Hegelian antithesis of being, a stationary datum. Nihilism is disappointed seriousness turned back against itself. [...] It appears either at the moment of adolescence, when the individual, seeing his child's universe flow away, feels the lack which is in his heart, or, later on, when the attempts to fulfill himself as a being have failed; in any case, among men who wish to rid themselves of the anxiety of their freedom by denying the world and themselves.[11]

De Beauvoir conceives of nihilism as a "radical disorder," as an "attitude," as "annihilation" of oneself, and as a way to get rid of "anxiety" by "denying" existence, all of which she sums up by defining nihilism as "disappointed seriousness turned back against itself." Nietzsche defined nihilism as the "highest values devaluing themselves." De Beauvoir is here echoing Nietzsche's definition, as the serious man who wanted to find proof that life is meaningful cannot find such proof, and in his disappointment he ends up rejecting meaningfulness as such.

Children become serious when they find that the world lacks the meaning they expected to find within it. Having conceived of meaningfulness as something to be discovered, as something that can be found in things, the child becomes a serious person in search of an external authority that can fill the void left by the lack of meaning in the world. But because the serious person conceives of meaning in such black-and-white, either/or terms, the serious person who cannot find an external authority can no longer find the world to be meaningful. Disappointed serious people thus come to reject the serious world that they formerly embraced and end up embracing meaninglessness instead, for in a world with no external authority the disappointed serious person prefers the annihilation of nihilism to the anxiety of freedom.

To say that nihilism is "disappointed seriousness turned back against itself" is to say that the logic of seriousness—if there is an external authority, then everything matters—culminates in the logic of nihilism—if there is no external authority, then nothing matters. Nihilism is thus an antidote to the anxiety of freedom because it severs freedom from responsibility and so severs freedom from anxiety. If there is no external authority to make our decisions meaningful, then the nihilist concludes that our decisions don't matter, and so rather than be anxious, we should just try to relax and be carefree. In other words, to be a nihilist is to live life as prescribed by Tartaglia and Lin-Chi.

From the perspective of nihilism there is no point in worrying about freedom if all choices end up leading to the same destination: death. The nihilist sees death as proof

of the meaninglessness of freedom and therefore of existence. Without an external authority that can guarantee
that we can evade the finality of death, that can guarantee
that our actions have meaning beyond our minuscule life
spans, existence appears as a cruel joke with freedom as
the punchline. The serious person didn't get the joke, but
the nihilist does, and so the nihilist is willing to stop being
serious and to just laugh along.

To be a serious person is to try to escape anxiety by
outsourcing the responsibility of freedom to an external
authority. To be a nihilist is to try to annihilate anxiety by
annihilating freedom, and to do so by denying the meaningfulness of decision-making. To give an example of such
nihilistic annihilation, de Beauvoir refers to Nazism, as nihilists cannot deny the meaning of their own decisions ("I
was just following orders") without also wanting to deny
the meaning of everyone else's decisions ("They were just
born impure"). The freedom of others is a threat to the
nihilist since confronting the freedom of others is to be
forced to confront one's own freedom, which would require confronting one's own responsibility, which would
bring back one's own anxiety. The existence of freedom
anywhere is a threat to the nihilist's desire for the nonex-
istence of freedom everywhere.

Of course, the attempt to annihilate freedom need
not, and most often does not, take the form of mass
murder. Freedom can be annihilated—as is described by

existentialism—by thinking of death as not worth worrying about, by thinking we should try to enjoy life instead of being needlessly morbid. Freedom can also be annihilated—as is described by postmodernism—by thinking of meaning as not worth worrying about, by thinking we should just accept traditional meanings instead of making life needlessly complicated. De Beauvoir thus makes clear why existentialism and postmodernism need not be seen as at odds with each other, since what postmodernism identifies as nihilism is not taking the meaning of meaning seriously, and what existentialism identifies as nihilism is not taking the meaning of death seriously. We can now see then that existentialism and postmodernism are merely identifying different forms nihilism can take, different ways in which "disappointed seriousness turned back against itself."

This is not to say though that we are acting nihilistically whenever we don't take something seriously. There are certainly plenty of things that need not be taken seriously, like fantasy football, the British royal family, or Ayn Rand. But nihilism is not the end result of a process of determining something's seriousness. Rather, as de Beauvoir suggests by likening nihilism to a "radical disorder," to be nihilistic is to deny the possibility of seriousness and to do so instinctively in a way similar to what Freud meant by a "defense mechanism." If you are caught eating cake at 2 a.m. and you say, "My genetic predisposition to snacking made me do it," then you're engaging in seriousness. But if you are caught eating cake at 2 a.m. and you say, "What's the big deal? It's just a piece of cake," then you're engaging in nihilism.

The nihilist does not try to defend actions like the serious person does by giving reasons that point to an external authority that could justify actions as meaningful. Rather, the nihilist—having turned seriousness against itself—does not see actions as capable of being defended and so undermines the practice of reason-giving itself. When challenged to defend their actions, nihilists turn the tables and force challengers to defend why they think there was anything in the actions worth being upset over. Nihilists appear to engage in rational arguments, but appearances are deceiving, as instead they weaponize rationality in order to make arguing purposeless.

Kierkegaard warned that reflection, when engaged in to a pathological degree, can lead to paralysis on both an individual and a cultural level. In his work *The Present Age* (1846), Kierkegaard writes,

> ... the present generation, wearied by its chimerical efforts, relapses into complete indolence. Its condition is that of a man who has only fallen asleep towards morning: first of all come great dreams, then a feeling of laziness, and finally a witty or clever excuse for remaining in bed. [...] Instead of coming

to his help, his *milieu* forms around him a negative intellectual opposition, which juggles for a moment with a deceptive prospect, only to deceive him in the end by pointing to a brilliant way out of the difficulty—by showing him that the shrewdest thing of all is to do nothing.[12]

Similarly, the German-American philosopher Hannah Arendt viewed nihilism as a way of thinking that can look rational but is really an attack on the purpose of rationality. Just as de Beauvoir defined nihilism as *seriousness turned against seriousness*, Arendt defined nihilism as *thinking turned against thinking*. In her final work, *The Life of the Mind* (1978), Arendt writes,

What we commonly call "nihilism"—and are tempted to date historically, decry politically, and ascribe to thinkers who allegedly dared to think "dangerous thoughts"—is actually a danger inherent in the thinking activity itself. There are no dangerous thoughts; thinking itself is dangerous, but nihilism is not its product. Nihilism is but the other side of conventionalism; its creed consists of negations of the current so-called positive values, to which it remains bound. All critical examinations must go through a stage of at least hypothetically negating accepted opinions and "values" by searching out their implications and tacit assumptions, and in this sense nihilism may be seen as an ever-present danger of thinking.

But that danger does not arise out of the Socratic conviction that the unexamined life is not worth living, but, on the contrary, out of the desire to find results that would make further thinking unnecessary. Thinking is equally dangerous to all creeds and, by itself, does not bring forth any new creed. Its most dangerous aspect from the viewpoint of common sense is that what was meaningful while you were thinking dissolves the moment you want to apply it to everyday life.[13]

We can see what Arendt means by describing nihilism as arising out of "the desire to find results that would make further thinking unnecessary" by looking at one typical table-turning strategy employed by nihilists: taking such a microscopic and decontextualized view of actions as to make them seem too ridiculous to care about. For example, reducing an offensive joke to just a couple of words put together to produce laughter, or reducing sex to just a couple of bodies put together to produce pleasure. Since no one would think of themselves as opposed to laughter or to pleasure, the nihilist's perspective can be very convincing, and so any further thought on the matter is made unnecessary. In this way nihilists are able to make serious people question the legitimacy not only of their feelings but of their seriousness. In other words, nihilism is "dangerous" not only because it is self-destructive but also because it can be *contagious*.

The idea that nihilism can be contagious is useful for understanding what may seem like a tension between Nietzsche's description of nihilism as a cultural phenomenon and de Beauvoir's description of nihilism as an individual attitude. Nihilism in an individual is a disorder, but nihilism in a society is a disease. The search of the serious for an external authority to give life meaning is not an individual endeavor. As Lyotard described, such a search is based on *metanarratives*, on practices and on concepts that have a history, a history that a serious person is born into and thus does not create but only adopts and perpetuates. This is why nihilism can be so contagious, as the disappointed serious person does not turn against a seriousness that is personal, but a seriousness that is cultural.

The arguments of the nihilist are convincing to those around the nihilist because the arguments are based on the logic of seriousness shared by those around the nihilist. In particular, nihilists often focus on the means/ends logic of seriousness. Seriousness seeks out external authority, but the external authority is a means to the serious person's end, which, as we have already seen, is the ability to enjoy life like a child rather than to be filled with anxiety like an adult. The nihilist thus offers the serious person a way to achieve this end without having to worry about the means. To the extent that the nihilist succeeds in enjoying life like a child, it is not from finding a new parent as the serious person believes is required, but simply from adopting the uncaring attitude of a child. In other words, nihilism is like consequentialism, only without the pesky concern about consequences.

When the contagion of nihilism spreads, we come to increasingly see the world the way a sick person does, wanting only what we think will make us feel better and avoiding anything that we think will make us feel worse. Consequently, external authority figures like scientists come to be judged not by facts but by feelings. We readily believe those who tell us what we want to hear ("A glass of wine a day will make you live longer") and reject those who tell us what we don't want to hear ("We need to drastically reduce our carbon emissions to protect the environment"). So while nihilism can make us as carefree and happy as children, it can also make us as careless and destructive as children. Nihilism is therefore the ability to enjoy a glass of wine while watching the world burn.

WHERE IS NIHILISM?

Now that we have developed in the previous chapters a more detailed analysis of what nihilism is, we can begin to develop in this chapter an analysis of where nihilism is. Nihilism is not merely the denial that life is inherently meaningful, as nihilism can instead be seen as a particular way of responding to the anxiety caused by the discovery of life's inherent meaninglessness. The nihilist does not despair like the pessimist, detest like the cynic, nor detach like the apathetic individual. Nihilists can be optimistic, idealistic, and sympathetic, as their aim in life is to be happy, to be as happy and carefree as they were when they were children, as happy and carefree as they were before they discovered that life lacked the meaning they thought they'd find in it when they grew up.

As we have seen, the nihilist's way of responding to life's meaninglessness cannot be properly understood if reduced to an individual affair. On the one hand, nihilism is like a disease, a contagious attitude that can quickly spread from individual to individual. On the other hand, nihilism is contagious because the nihilistic way of life is an outgrowth of a way of life that nihilists are born into and share with others.

Considering the danger of being surrounded by people who do not care about the consequences of their actions, we might expect that society would be actively engaged in combating nihilism. Yet while the label of "nihilist" is used in everyday life as a term of criticism, the logic of nihilism can nevertheless be found to be championed by various elements of society. Hence, the spread of nihilism might not only be due to the contagiousness of a nihilistic attitude among individuals but might also be due to cultural influences that encourage a nihilistic attitude and help to make it so contagious. And it is just such cultural influences that this chapter will explore, as nihilism can be found on TV, in the classroom, on the job, and in politics.

Nihilism at Home

Given that nihilism results from the desire to become free from the anxiety of freedom, it should perhaps not surprise us that contemporary pop culture would embrace nihilism—for if we turn to pop culture in order to be entertained, to be comforted, to be distracted, then pop culture already shares with nihilism at the very least the aim of stress reduction. Yet what should concern us about pop culture is not whether it attracts nihilists, but whether it helps to motivate people to become nihilistic.

Parents have long worried about the corrupting influences of pop culture, such as whether watching television can make children dumber or whether playing video games can make children more violent. Such concerns tend to focus on the content of pop culture rather than on the devices through which we consume pop culture. One reason for this is that watching a screen has become so normal that we no longer question this way of spending our time. In other words, we ask people *what* they're watching, but we don't ask people *why* they're watching.

Watching as a leisure activity has of course existed since long before the existence of screens. However, with screens, we no longer need to go somewhere to watch something. The philosopher Günther Anders argued in his 1956 essay "The World as Phantom and as Matrix" that radio and television were helping to create what he called "the mass man."[1] Radio and television programs fill the home with conversation, with the conversation of others, making the conversation of those consuming those programs not only difficult but a nuisance. Moreover, television sets structure the layout of furniture so that everyone can watch, requiring that people don't sit facing each other, but sit facing the screen. As the events consumed are recorded and replayed for consumption, radio and television not only make it unnecessary to leave the house in order to witness events but also lead to events being staged such that they can be recorded and replayed for consumption. So rather than providing us experiences of real life, radio and television provide us with a pseudo-reality (events staged for mass consumption) that we can pseudo-experience (consumption from our couches) in our pseudo-lives (consuming near others rather than being with others).

What is at issue for Anders is the way radio and television reshape what we think of as "experience," what we think of as "communication," and even what we think of as "intimacy." We form relationships with characters in programs in ways that we do not form relationships with characters on a stage, as radio and television put characters in intimate proximity to us, making it seem as though they are talking to us, as though they are letting us into their homes just as we are letting them into ours. As the philosopher Theodor Adorno similarly argued in his 1954 essay "How to Look at Television,"[2] such intimacy makes it easy for us to identify with television characters, particularly as they are portrayed in familiar settings, in familiar situations, in familiar conflicts. And yet though these characters may have jobs, families, and problems that resemble our own, their lives have a stability and security that in no way resembles our lives.

The sitcom family may get into trouble, but within 30 minutes (22 if you're counting commercial breaks) the trouble will be resolved. Whatever disorder may have erupted to create both comic and dramatic tension will disappear, likely to never be brought up again, and order will be restored. Formulaic programming is thus deeply comforting, as it helps us to feel that situations that seem worth worrying about will work out for the best in the end, that the consequences of our actions don't really matter. And it is of course precisely such need for comfort that brings us to screens to watch formulaic programming.

But that we know such programming is comforting does not mean that we know what else such programming may be doing to us. Adorno's concern was that, along with our being comforted, such programs were also helping to induce in us a feeling of complacency, as what is comforting is specifically the return by the end of each episode to the status quo. Television therefore not only entertains us but also teaches us. Preservation of the status quo is *good*. Disruption of the status quo is *bad*.

Of course, in the age of prestige TV, it may seem that such analyses are outdated. Perhaps the programs that Anders and Adorno were watching in the 1950s were formulaic and reinforced a sense of complacency, but today's TV shows are supposed to be complicated works of art made to resemble literature, not made to keep people staring at a screen between soap commercials. Yet while prestige programs like *Breaking Bad*, *Mad Men*, and *Game of Thrones* certainly do not use formulas that people who grew up watching TV would recognize, that doesn't mean that these shows are not formulaic. Walter White kept breaking bad. Don Draper kept breaking promises. Lannisters kept breaking Starks. Prestige programs create their own formulas, formulas that the audience expects the show to adhere to, formulas that subsequent shows try to copy in order to piggyback off the original show's success.

While these shows might not be selling soap, they are still in the business of keeping people staring at screens. Whereas traditional programming often tried to present a wholesome and idyllic dreamworld that was a better version of reality, contemporary programming often presents nightmare versions of reality meant to scare us from ever wanting to go outside again. In either version of programming what is important is the idea that screens offer an escape from reality, and reality is implicitly or explicitly presented as that from which we must escape.

In the era of binge-watching and handheld screens, the business of escapism—the business of keeping people staring at screens—is only getting more and more successful. Evading reality though staring at screens has become the status quo, the status quo that screens train us to conform to and to be complacent about, the status

In the era of binge-watching and handheld screens, the business of escapism—the business of keeping people staring at screens—is only getting more and more successful.

quo that we have come to accept as good to preserve and as bad to disrupt. Whereas previously staring at screens was treated as doing nothing, as being a "couch potato" in front of a "boob tube," now, thanks to the aura of "prestige" and "critical acclaim," staring at screens not only is considered to be doing something but is increasingly becoming the only way we know how to do anything.

Nihilism at School

Staring at screens has become so commonplace that when someone asks us to look up from our screens, we often get confused and angry. This may occur, for example, when a teacher asks students to put their phones away. Though, of course, when the teacher tells students to stop staring at screens and to pay attention in class, that often means the students just need to stop looking at *their screens* and instead look at *the teacher's screen*, at the giant screen in front of the class that everyone can stare at together.

The screen may be a chalkboard or a PowerPoint presentation, but even in the classroom there is still the expectation that all eyes need to be on a screen. The teacher is thus like a television executive fighting against competing content on competing screens for the attention of the audience. And like a television executive, the teacher often uses well-worn formulas (e.g., the "Socratic method") in order to present content in a way that will be most appealing to the audience and in a way that will be most easy for the audience to absorb.

The Brazilian philosopher, activist, and educator Paulo Freire was very concerned about the expectation that teachers should be content deliverers and students should be content absorbers. In his 1968 work *Pedagogy of the Oppressed*, Freire argues, "Education is suffering from narration sickness."[3] When teachers are trained to educate by talking at students, and students are trained to be educated by passively listening to teachers, learning is reduced to repetition. In order to be successful, students need only repeat back to the teacher what they have heard from the teacher and what they have read from the reading assigned by the teacher. It would thus not be surprising to Freire that we now frequently use phrases like "artificial intelligence," "smart devices," and "machine learning" to talk about technology, as students have been treated like machines for so long it would only be natural that we would start treating machines like students.

Freire uses the metaphor of a bank to describe what narration sickness does to learning. Students are expected to listen passively to teachers because it is taken for granted that teachers have information and students do not. Information is a form of currency, a currency that teachers deposit into the minds of students. Students are thus thought of as empty receptacles—or banks—waiting to be filled. Such a view gives rise to a teacher/student relationship that is necessarily hierarchical, as teachers are expected to be informed experts, and students are expected to be uninformed novices. This relationship gives rise to a dynamic where teachers are all-powerful and students are all powerless, as teachers have the power to instruct as they please and to punish as they please while students are left with no option but to obey or leave.

The issue here for Freire is not that it is wrong to think teachers have more information than students, but rather that it is wrong to think that education is merely a process of information exchange. So long as information is what is valued by society, so long as learning is only seen by society as a form of economic transaction, then it makes sense for schools to use a top-down model of education. What information *means* may become increasingly irrelevant, but all that matters is that information is *possessed*. And because the possession of information is all that matters, not only are students motivated to plagiarize but students even argue that plagiarism should be seen as legitimate since it's the best way to guarantee that the information they possess is correct.

Of course, it is hard to refute student arguments that plagiarism is wrong when the model of education in which they find themselves encourages an instrumental attitude toward learning. As we have seen, this instrumentality can be found not only in treating learning as a means to an end rather than as an end in itself but also in treating students and teachers as instruments of information storage and distribution. Learning is still spoken of in schools using the same hallowed language that has always surrounded it, giving it the aura of something intrinsically good. But because the language of learning does not match the practice of learning, students simply come to see education as hollow and school as a chore. And if students don't reach such conclusions on their own, then schools provide standardized testing in order to guarantee that students see schooling as nothing but a process of standardizing human beings.

When students all have to learn the same information in the same way, creativity and diversity are discouraged while obedience and conformity are not only encouraged but required. As Freire writes,

> It is not surprising that the banking concept of education regards men as adaptable, manageable beings. The more students work at storing the deposits entrusted to them, the less they develop the critical consciousness which would result from their intervention in the world as transformers of that world. The more completely they accept the passive role imposed on them, the more they tend simply to adapt to the world as it is and to the fragmented

view of reality deposited in them. [...] Indeed, the interests of the oppressors lie in "changing the consciousness of the oppressed, not the situation which oppresses them"; for the more the oppressed can be led to adapt to that situation, the more easily they can be dominated.[4]

As Freire argues, treating the goal of education as information regurgitation prevents students from developing the ability to think critically. While such a lack of critical development would seem like a failing of the banking model of education, Freire suggests that it should instead be seen as proof that this education system is working precisely as designed.

According to Freire, students are not learning how to criticize society but instead only how to conform to society. For this reason Freire argues that the banking model of education is an oppressive system designed by oppressors to teach the oppressed to accept their oppression. Freire's argument against education is thus parallel to Nietzsche's argument against morality. In both cases the problem is not that society is failing to create good citizens, but that what is meant by "good" is what is good *for society* rather than what is good *for humans*, for the people who have to live in the society sustained by these educational and moral systems.

The "narration sickness" identified by Freire can now be seen as the sickness Nietzsche identified as nihilism. The status quo is protected by valuing conformity as what is good, a value that is reinforced by receiving "good grades" for "good work." Such moralistic language further reinforces conformity by entangling educational values with moral values, making clear to students that they should feel pride when they are obedient ("good student") and guilt when they are disobedient ("bad student"). Students who plagiarize are thus often told that what they are doing is *wrong* because it runs counter to moral values, because plagiarizing is *cheating*, and cheating is something done by people who have a *bad character*.

The education system may be designed in such a way that it leads students to see plagiarism as perfectly reasonable given what is expected of them. But morality is designed in such a way that it protects the education system by making students feel personally responsible for plagiarism. Because the banking model of education prevents students from developing critical thinking, students are less likely to recognize the degree to which the education system itself is responsible for making plagiarism seem reasonable. And if they are able to question the education system, they are labeled as "troublemakers" and punished for having been "disrespectful" of their teachers. In other words, because what is currently valued as education has devalued education, morality is required to step in and fill the void, reinforcing hollowed out educational values (e.g., learning for the sake of learning) with moral values (e.g., learning for the sake of duty).

As Nietzsche warned, a society that only values its own survival, that only values the protection of the status quo, is a sick society, a society that creates *good citizens* but *bad humans*. Likewise Freire argues that the oppressiveness of the banking model of education is dehumanizing both for the oppressors and for the oppressed. For Freire, learning requires being able to have a dialogue, but to have a dialogue the participants must regard each other as equals in order to speak *with* each other rather than *at* each other. Reducing learning to the depositing of information prevents both teachers and students from being able to communicate with each other as equals rather than as merely the informed and the uninformed. Top-down information-centric education thus prevents human beings from being able to see each other as human beings, which in turn prevents both teachers and students from being able to genuinely learn from each other by being able to enter into dialogue with each other.

This lack of genuine learning is detrimental not only to students and to teachers but to society as a whole. While the banking model of education may be useful for preserving the status quo of society, it is detrimental for the future of society. As Nietzsche warned, social preservation

As Nietzsche warned, a society that only values its own survival, that only values the protection of the status quo, is a sick society, a society that creates *good citizens* but *bad humans*.

merely creates social stagnation and, ultimately, social destruction. Education, like entertainment, can be used to make life easier and more stable, but if challenge and uncertainty are required for growth, then an easy and stable life is really just a slow and steady death. In other words, such a life is nihilistic.

Nihilism at Work

A likely counterargument to Freire's criticisms of the banking model of education is that he simply did not appreciate that the true purpose of education is to prepare students for *the real world*. The real world is top-down. The real world is information-centric. So if students were taught in the way that Freire advocated, taught to think of authority figures not as their superiors but as their equals, taught to be critical of conformity and to question rather than follow rules, they would simply be forced to suffer a rude awakening when they finished school and tried to get a job. In other words, the banking model of education isn't *nihilistic*, it's *realistic*.

Such a view of the relationship between education and employment is hard to argue against, as surely we need a particular kind of schooling to prepare students for the particular kind of working that they are most likely to enter into. But this argument of course raises the question of why we have come to accept this particular kind of working if it would require this particular kind of schooling. For if Freire is right that the way we teach students is dehumanizing and the counterargument is not that Freire is wrong but that we teach students in this manner because it prepares them for the real world, then this counterargument is really just another way of saying that *the real world is dehumanizing* and that we should just *learn to accept it*.

The idea that what we have come to accept as *the real world* is a world of dehumanizing work is an idea that was argued for most influentially by Karl Marx. In his essay "Alienated Labor," an essay that Marx never finished nor published, we can find the philosophical underpinnings of Marx's criticisms of capitalism. In the essay Marx analyzes the various ways in which trying to make money can end up making us less human, and the various ways in which we become blinded by money so that we also end up caring more about the dream of being rich than the reality of not being human.

According to Marx, "labor" is a process by which we make objects, objects that we need in order to find out who we are. When a child builds a sandcastle and desperately tries to make her dad look up from his screen in order to see what she built, she's trying to get her dad not just to appreciate the sandcastle but also to appreciate her. Or to be more specific, the dad's appreciation of his daughter's sandcastle *is* his appreciation of her. In building the sandcastle, she has put herself into the sandcastle, and so her dad's judgment of what she made is his judgment of her. We make sandcastles to find out if we're creative, we make jokes to find out if we're funny, and we make conversation to find out if we're interesting. We make things to find out who we are because we identify ourselves in and through what we make.

In a feudal society where goods were exchanged through barter, people would have come to know each other through each other's labor. Making things is thus not only how we find out who we ourselves are but also how we find out who others are. Labor is then necessary not only for discovering one's own identity but also for building a community. The relationship between labor, identity, and community can be seen perhaps most clearly in the prevalence of the name Smith. Blacksmiths, goldsmiths, silversmiths, and so forth were known to the rest of their communities for their smithing and so came to be known as Smith (or its etymological cousin in other languages, such as Schmidt, Kowalski, Kovac, Ferraro, Herrera, and Faber). Likewise we still have today other such common occupationally suggestive names as Abbott, Archer, Baker, Barber, Carpenter, Cook, Farmer, Fisher, Glazer, Glover, Hunter, Judge, Knight, Mason, Painter, Shepherd, Tanner, and Taylor, to name a few. In other words, labor is so fundamental to identity that the labor of one's ancestors can continue to define one's family for generations.

It is due to this essential relationship between identity and labor that Marx focuses his attention on the rise of industrialization through the division of labor. The move from labor being performed by individual craftsmen to labor being performed by multiple people working on an assembly line certainly helped to make production faster and more efficient. However, to simply call this "progress" is to ignore what the division of labor does to the laborers. While we often focus our concerns about industrialization on the horrible working conditions in factories, Marx instead makes clear how the division of labor is itself detrimental to laborers. Working conditions can be improved, but by cutting labor up into tasks, tasks that can be performed mindlessly for hours on end, laborers became divided from their labor, and so became divided from their identity.

A crisis of identity arises therefore when we lose control over what we make. As Charlie Chaplin illustrated in the movie *Modern Times* (1936), workers on an assembly line make parts of parts of parts, working without knowing what they're working on or why, thus becoming just another cog in a machine. And as Mike Judge illustrated in the movie *Office Space* (1999), moving from an assembly line to a cubicle has not helped alleviate the cog-like feeling of work and has perhaps even made it worse. For now that we have improved working conditions, now that we have health care, 40-hour work weeks, sick leave, vacation time, photocopiers, and coffee machines, there is increasingly little left for us to hate about work other than *working itself*.

Industrialization and subsequent revolutions in production have turned labor from a source of identity to a source of misery. The sense of community produced by labor no longer comes from sharing our creations with each other, but only comes from sharing our hatred of work with each other. This is why Marx described contemporary labor in terms of "alienation,"[5] for as the products of our labor become alien to us, so we become alien to ourselves, to each other, and to what it means to be human. We cannot help but define ourselves through what we make, but ever since the Industrial Revolution "what we make" has come to mean only "how much money we make." We are defined then not by showing others who we are, but by showing others our paychecks.

To become defined by a paycheck is to become defined by what one can consume rather than by what one can create, replacing pride in what we make with pride in what we own. We work in order to make money, renting out our minds and our bodies to the highest bidder. Minds and bodies are then no longer who we are, they are merely means at our disposal for making money and thus need have no more meaning for us than employees have for a CEO. Mind/body dualism is then not merely a metaphysical theory, it is also an effective management strategy.

A great way to succeed at making money is to *internalize* the division of labor. By trying to divide ourselves into physical selves and mental selves, we can maximize the output of the former and minimize the input of the latter. However, as Marx explains, being able to increase our work output comes at high cost:

> What, then, constitutes the alienation of labor? First, in the fact that labor is *external* to the worker, that is, that it does not belong to his essential being; that in his work, therefore, he does not affirm himself but denies himself, does not feel well but unhappy, does not freely develop his physical and mental energy but mortifies his body and ruins his mind. The worker, therefore, feels himself only outside his work, and feels beside himself in his work. He is at home when he is not working, and when he is working he is not at home. His work therefore is not voluntary, but coerced; it is *forced labor*. It is therefore not the satisfaction of a need, but only a *means* for satisfying needs external to it. Its alien character emerges clearly in the fact that labor is shunned like the plague as soon as there is no physical or other compulsion.[6]

In other words, it is much easier to get through each workday if we can *do* our jobs without having to be *aware* of what we're doing. Whether working on a factory floor or on an Excel spreadsheet, thought, reflection, and consciousness are often detrimental to our ability to survive work. The more automatic work can be, the more zombielike we can be at work. And the more zombielike we can be at work, the less work *feels like work* because zombies *don't feel at all*.

If we spend a third of our lives sleeping, and we spend our time at work trying to put ourselves to sleep, then for most of our lives we aren't just *acting* like zombies, we *are* zombies. To be a worker, to have to work for a living, is to be—as George A. Romero made clear in multiple subtext-rich movies—a member of the living dead. We are happiest when we can deaden our minds at work and deaden our bodies after work, for which reason we call the hour after work, the hour we spend "eating, drinking, procreating"[7] ourselves into a stupor, our *happy hour*.

Of course, as Marx makes clear, even if labor no longer serves the purpose it had as "the satisfaction of a need," labor is not purposeless, as it is now "a *means* for satisfying needs external to it." We do not zombify ourselves for nothing, but in order to be able to afford to eat, to drink, and to procreate. The problem that Marx is pointing to here then is not that labor has become meaningless, but rather that, even though labor has become alienating and dehumanizing, we still find it meaningful enough to keep doing it. The meaning of labor has been replaced with the

To be a worker, to have to work for a living, is to be—as George A. Romero made clear in multiple subtext-rich movies—a member of the living dead.

meaning of money. However, money is a piece of metal, or a piece of paper, or (more recently) a piece of code, something that is itself meaningless beyond the ability to exchange it for goods and services. The goods and services we can buy with the money we get from our labor must then be what drive us to keep laboring after our labor has become meaningless.

But because these goods and services are produced by laborers like us, laborers who are themselves working not for the sake of work but for the sake of money, then these goods and services have also lost the meaning they once had. Goods are mass produced and thus no longer provide any way to identify the individuality of their maker. Services may still be provided with a smile, but not because they still represent a genuine human interaction, but because service industry workers are trained by bosses to smile to avoid being fired, and trained by customers to smile to earn a tip.

Goods and services are then not meaningful because through them we learn about the people providing them, but are meaningful because of how they make us feel to have them. We might no longer care about who makes our food or who fixes our plumbing, but we still need to eat and to shower. And as we become able to afford better food and better showers, we become able to move from merely satisfying needs to instead fulfilling desires. It is the promise of being able to fulfill our desires that motivates us to keep working long after working has itself ceased to be either fulfilling or desirable. Labor is not in itself meaningful. Money we get from labor is not in itself meaningful. The goods and services we get from money are not in themselves meaningful. But the feeling of fulfillment we get from goods and services is meaningful.

This new meaning of labor that Marx is describing can be seen, however, to operate on the premise that *to be human* is *to be empty*. For if we are fulfilled not through what we do, but through what we can buy, through the goods and services that we can acquire, then without those goods and services, we are nothing. We are no longer able to fulfill ourselves, we no longer find our own creations to be desirable. Instead we seek fulfillment from acquisition and consumption because what we can acquire and consume is desirable. But if, as Marx suggests, we were previously able to fulfill ourselves through what we could do rather than through what we could own, then the desire for acquisition and consumption is not natural, but is itself something we have acquired and consumed.

That these desires are not natural makes sense since often the desire we have for goods and services has nothing to do with the goods and services themselves. What we desire is the status those goods and services have in society and the status that we thereby attain through association with them. If certain goods and services are seen by society as luxurious, then to have such luxuries is to be seen by society as living a life of luxury. And if we can have a life that others desire, then we can feel ourselves to be desirable. But of course, as Eddie Murphy illustrated in *Coming to America* (1988), such desirability by association can be deceiving, as we can never know whether people who claim to desire us would continue to desire us if misfortunate fell and we no longer had any association with such desirable goods and services. In other words, such fulfillment still leaves us feeling empty.

Yet, as Socrates warn us at the end of Plato's *Republic*, such a feeling of emptiness does not lead us to realize that acquisition and consumption are actually unfulfilling pursuits. Instead this feeling leads us to endlessly pursue more and more acquisition and consumption. Plato writes,

> Therefore, those who have no experience of reason or virtue, but are always occupied with feasts and the like, are brought down and then back up to the middle, as it seems, and wander in this way throughout their lives, never reaching beyond this to what is truly higher up, never looking up at it or being brought up to it, and so they aren't filled with that which really is and never taste any stable or pure pleasure. They always look down at the table, they feed, fatten, and fornicate. To outdo others in these things, they kick and butt them with iron horns and hooves, killing each other, because their desires

are insatiable. For the part that they're trying to fill is like a vessel full of holes, and neither it nor the things they are trying to fill it with are among the things that are.[8]

If acquisition and consumption make us feel fulfilled—and if in the current world of work they are often the only things that make us feel fulfilled—then the fleetingness of that fulfillment will only make us more determined to acquire and consume as often as possible. As Plato makes clear, the people who would pursue such unfulfilling fulfillment are those "who have no experience of reason or virtue." In other words, if a life of acquisition and consumption is the only life we know, then we would not see a life of meaningless labor for meaningless money for meaningless goods and services for meaningless fulfillment as *a meaningless life*, instead we would see it as *the real world*.

As Marx concludes, if we have come to see a meaningless reality as *reality*, this is not because *reality is meaningless*, but because having workers accept meaninglessness as reality must be a benefit to someone else. As Marx writes,

If the product of labor does not belong to the worker, if it is an alien power that confronts him, then this is possible only because it belongs to *a man other than the worker*. If the worker's activity is torment for him, it must be *pleasure* and a joy of life for another. Neither the gods, nor nature, but only man himself can be this alien power over man.[9]

Having workers believe that they have no choice but to work for a living is a belief that clearly benefits people who do not work for a living, people who do not need to work for a living, at least so long as there are workers who they can live off of instead. The question that needs to be answered then is this: How and why did people accept this belief?

For Marx, the answer to this question is that workers were willing to work for a living because they believed the benefits (e.g., money) would outweigh the costs (e.g., dehumanization). For Plato, the answer to this question is that workers were willing to work for a living because they believed no other way of life was possible. So, to form such beliefs, the workers needed, on the one hand, to be able to alienate themselves from their humanity without worrying about the consequences, and on the other hand, to learn to conform to reality rather than question it. In other words, if you want people to accept the belief that working for a living is the only way to live, then you want people to accept nihilism.

If we can distract ourselves from what we are doing to ourselves—such as by staring at screens for hours on end every day—then we can work for a living without having to feel alive enough to care about the consequences. If we can be taught at school how to be compliant rather than be critical—such as by learning to accept that we are empty vessels and that authority figures have all the answers—then we can learn to accept that working for a living is not *nihilistic*, it is simply *normal*. Nihilism at home, nihilism at school, and nihilism at work are thus not different examples of the same *nihilistic attitude*; they are different parts of the same *nihilistic system*.

If we live in a nihilistic world, it is not because the world *is* nihilistic, but because the world we live in is perpetuated by our acceptance of nihilism. The more accepting of nihilism we become, the more susceptible to exploitation we become. If we believe that to be human is to be empty, that our lives are essentially meaningless, and that we need to acquire and consume to feel fulfilled, then trading our humanity for the ability to acquire and consume doesn't seem *dehumanizing*; it seems like *a bargain*. Nihilism is therefore not best understood as an individualistic experience to be found wherever nihilistic individuals go, but as an experience generated by a system that feeds off nihilism, by a system that extends into every facet of human life.

To claim that nihilism is simply true is to not merely make a claim *about* the nature of reality, it is to make a claim that helps to *shape* reality. Nihilism cannot be seen as solely a moral or a metaphysical position without ignoring its political dimensions. If helping people to accept the normalcy of nihilism serves to help people become exploited and dehumanized, then arguments that treat nihilism as either an individual failing or as a cosmic truth are arguments that serve exploitative and dehumanizing ends.

When we think of nihilism as a way to describe an individual's moral beliefs (or the lack thereof), we reduce nihilism to a matter that only individuals could resolve on their own. When we think of nihilism as a way to describe the universe's meaningfulness (or the lack thereof), we elevate nihilism to a matter that only gods could resolve on their own. Either way of thinking about nihilism thus prevents us from recognizing the need to confront nihilism as a matter that could only be resolved *collectively*, at the level between that of individuals and of gods, at the level of *the political*.

Nihilism at City Hall

The political relevance of nihilism was most clearly articulated by Hannah Arendt. In "Introduction *into* Politics" (1955)—a book that Arendt did not complete but that has since been published as a long essay—Arendt traces the history of the meaning of politics back to the Ancient Greek origins of the word. Arendt carries out this historical analysis in order to show us that what we think of as "politics" today is not what would have been meant by "politics" to Plato and Aristotle.

Today we tend to think of politics as governments, elections, borders, laws, militaries, taxes, domestic policies, foreign policies, and, of course, corruption. Or to put it another way, politics today is basically everything we elect representatives to think about so we don't have to. But in the time of Plato and Aristotle politics was instead seen as an activity, an activity that we engage in not as a means to an end but as an *end in itself*, an activity that defined what it means to be human.

The question that Arendt is trying to answer in this essay is this: "Does politics still have any meaning at all?"[10] For the Ancient Greeks, politics meant freedom. We might think that we today share this meaning of politics with the Ancient Greeks, as we think that politics is how to *protect* freedom. If we see ourselves as having been born free but also born vulnerable, then we see politics as a necessary evil, as an evil that is necessary only insofar as it helps us to live so that we can enjoy our freedom. Politics is for many a limit on our freedom, and so we imagine utopia would be a world that had no need for politics. As Arendt points out, such utopian thinking became especially prevalent after World War II, as the rise of totalitarianism and the development of the atomic bomb meant that politics became seen as not a way to protect freedom, but as a *threat* to freedom, as a threat to life itself.

For the Ancient Greeks, however, it would have made no sense to conceive of politics as either a way to protect freedom or as a threat to freedom, as for them politics *is* freedom. Politics was originally understood to be an activity engaged in by those who were capable of freeing themselves from what was seen as inhuman, for which reason to engage in politics was to be human. What was inhuman was coercion. To be forced to do something—whether by another person or by nature—was to live like an animal, like something less than human. Animals act out of necessity, but humans are capable of acting spontaneously without external influence. Or to put it another way, humans can *act*, but animals can only *react*. As Arendt points out, when Aristotle defines humans as political beings, he does not mean that humans have always been and always will be involved in politics, but rather that the beings who can engage in politics are the beings who are human. Ancient Greeks saw themselves—and *only* themselves—as human because they had achieved what others had not: the creation of the *polis*, of a space for politics.

Because our animal necessities—necessities like eating, drinking, and procreating—were seen as needs that were managed at home, the home was associated with coercion rather than with freedom. To be free thus required the ability to leave home, to leave behind the necessities of life that nature forces us to satisfy. In other words, to be free required someone else be enslaved. As Arendt writes,

> Unlike all forms of capitalist exploitation, which pursue primarily economic ends aimed at increasing wealth, the point of the exploitation of slaves in classical Greece was to liberate their masters entirely from labor so that they then might enjoy the freedom of the political arena. This liberation was accomplished by force and compulsion, and was based on the absolute rule that every head of household exercised over his house.[11]

Rather than see slaves as people who were dehumanized by their servitude, the Ancient Greeks saw anyone who was not like them, who was not the head of a household, as *born to serve*. And so, as Aristotle argued, slaves were those who could and should take care of the inhuman necessities of the home in order to allow those capable of being human the "leisure" to be human.

Leisure—or liberation from the chore of having to take care of one's needs and of one's home—was not then conceived of as freedom, but as a *precondition* for freedom. Having secured leisure for himself, the head of a household was able to leave the private realm of the home and enter the public realm of the polis. The polis enabled a space for politics, and thus for freedom, because it created a place outside the home where *citizens* (i.e., adult Greek men who were the head of a household) could meet and could speak.

To be a citizen was to regard other citizens, and to be regarded by other citizens, as an *equal*, as having the same standing in the polis. As such, a political space was a space where citizens could speak with equals and as equals. Equality therefore was nothing more than a result of the requirement that the polis be a space for freedom. For the Ancient Greeks, freedom meant freedom from coercion not only in the sense of freedom from natural necessities but also in the sense of freedom from hierarchical inequalities.

The inequalities that created the polis (Greek > non-Greek, husband > wife, father > child) were therefore what allowed for the creation of the equality (citizen = citizen) of the *agora*. The agora, or the public square, was the specific place in the polis where citizens could meet and speak to each other *freely*, without having to worry about satisfying needs or having to worry about issuing commands. Domestic affairs as well as foreign affairs were then seen by the Ancient Greeks as *unpolitical*.

Managing the economy or managing the military involves giving commands. Because commands require a relationship of speaker who commands and of listener who obeys, the speaking involved in commands would not have been equivalent to what the Ancient Greeks considered to be free speech. The agora was a political space because it was a space where citizens could be human, a space where citizens could be among equals, a space where citizens could be free *from* coercion and free *to* speak.

Freedom of speech was not for the Ancient Greeks a way to voice opinions, but a way to share a world. As no individual citizen could possibly have a view of the world that was complete, to try to form a complete view of the world required individual citizens to come together and discuss their limited perspectives of the world with each other. As Arendt writes,

> Only in the freedom of our speaking with one another does the world, as that about which we speak, emerge in its objectivity and visibility from all sides. Living in a real world and speaking with one another about it are basically one and the same, and to the Greeks, private life seemed "idiotic" because it lacked the diversity that comes with speaking about something and thus the experience of how things really function in the world.[12]

If the home was the private domain for satisfying animalistic needs, then the agora was the public domain for satisfying human curiosities.

Though we have not retained this view of politics in our actions, we have retained it in our language, such as when we describe politics as "consensus building." To reach a "consensus" is to have come to share a view (-*sensus*) of the world with (*con-*) others. Similarly, we take for granted today that political agreements should be based on "common sense." Though we might not realize it, this idea refers back to the concept of the *sensus communis*, which can be understood epistemologically as a judgment based on one's own senses being in agreement, or politically as a judgment based on the sense experience of the members of a community being in agreement.

This is why the Ancient Greeks saw privacy and solitude as *idiotic*, as remaining closed off from the world, as staying silently within one's own limited worldview. Citizens were seen as needing to join together to collectively expand their views in order to avoid having views of reality that were incomplete and incoherent, to avoid having views that were merely *idiosyncratic*. In other words, if politics means freedom, and freedom means becoming human, then an individual cannot become human alone. Becoming human is a *political project*, a project that is essentially *public* and *collaborative*. Or as Aristotle put it, "a human being is by nature a social being."[13]

We can now see why for the Ancient Greeks politics would have been an end in itself rather than a means to an end. Politics was not originally about protecting life so that we could *individually* enjoy our freedom, it was about creating freedom so that *collectively* life could be made meaningful. This is what I take to be the core of Arendt's analysis in this essay. In the modern era we have greatly increased the number of people who can participate in politics, but because we have greatly reduced the scope of politics, we have made such participation *meaningless*.

Arendt traces the reduction of the meaning of politics back to Plato. For Plato, *truth* was distinct from, and superior to, *consensus*. Plato argued that the political debate of *the many* could never reach truth as human experience did not belong to the realm of truth. Plato sought to create a space outside of the political realm where *the few* could engage in a more truthful form of debate, what Plato called the "dialectic" of philosophy as opposed to the "rhetoric" of politics. Whereas the agora was a place in the polis where any head of household could participate in discussions about the nature of *experience*, Plato's Academy was a place within the polis meant to make the agora obsolete, a place where only his students would be able to participate in discussions about the nature of *reality*.

Though it was not political as it was not public, the Academy was still intended to be a space where participants could be free to speak by being free from coercion. To achieve such freedom, Plato and his students required the polis to provide them with the leisure necessary to leave the agora, just as the heads of households required slaves to provide them with the leisure necessary to leave the home. Hence, just as slavery was seen by the Ancient Greeks as a means to the end of political freedom, so politics was seen by Plato as a means to the end of *academic freedom*.

According to Arendt, Plato's creation of "academic freedom" was an idea that had a much greater impact on politics than did his advocacy for a "philosopher-king," as the former, unlike the latter, has actually been put into practice.[14] What is important about the concept of academic freedom is that it requires freedom from coercion not only in the sense of freedom from necessities and freedom from inequalities but also freedom from coercion in the sense of *freedom from politics*.

Plato elevated the truth-seeking activity of philosophy above the consensus-building activity of politics, an elevation that he argued for quite literally by likening participation in the public realm of politics to being held prisoner in an underground cave. By arguing that academic freedom was necessary to reach truth, and that academic freedom meant freedom from politics, Plato established a separation between truth and politics. Truth could only be reached by philosophers if politics was not allowed to interfere with philosophy, just as previously it was believed that consensus could be reached by citizens only if domesticity was not allowed to interfere with politics.

After Plato, both political activities and domestic activities came to be seen as activities that were not in themselves meaningful, but that were means to the end of meaningful activity. The Ancient Greek creation of political space as a space for meaningful activity entailed the treatment of domestic space as a space for meaningless activity. Plato's creation of academic space served, however, as a challenge to the meaningfulness of political space, bringing political activities down to the level of domestic activities.

Domestic activities and political activities both had in common that they were activities based entirely on human experience. Plato argued that, since human experience was particular rather than universal, and was always changing rather than permanent, human experience lacked the essential qualities of universality and of permanence that defined truth. Thus, if truth determined what was meaningful, then meaningful activity was not to be found in the home nor in the agora; it could be found only in the Academy.

In Plato's *Apology* we find the claim that "the unexamined life is not worth living." We can now see that this claim was not meant to be understood as a call for everyone to join the Academy, since of course there would then have been no one left in the home or in the agora to take care of the domestic and political activities that made the Academy possible. Rather, the unexamined life makes the examined life possible, so its worth is not intrinsic, but instrumental. According to Plato, unexamined lives are in themselves worthless, but they are nevertheless necessary since they still contribute to that which is worthwhile: the "harmony"[15] of the polis.

Such harmony was to be achieved when everyone in the polis was doing what they were born to do. According to Plato's "Myth of the Metals"[16]—which today might be better known as J. K. Rowling's "Myth of the Sorting Hat"—one's place in the polis was supposed to be capable of being determined by the nature of one's soul. Thus, whether one led an examined or an unexamined life was not a matter of choice, but of birth. Rather, the only choice that did matter, according to Plato, was whether individuals would choose to carry out their fated tasks in life or if they would instead rebel by trying to take on a role in the polis other than the one that they were told they were born to perform.

Whereas the Ancient Greeks kept people in their place by using the threat of death, Plato instead used the threat of *disharmony*. With the "Myth of Gyges"[17] Plato argued that someone who abandoned his role in the polis to become richer and more powerful would *appear* to be happy satisfying all of his desires. But because his soul would be in disharmony from having let his desires rather than his reason rule him, *in reality* his soul would be suffering. Plato thus likened disharmony to a disease, a disease that was *invisible*, for which reason we are blind to its corrupting influence on the soul and on the polis and so require philosophers to diagnose it. We are consequently led by

Plato to trust philosophers rather than our own experience, since to trust our senses is to run the risk of mistakenly believing that the *visible appearance* of happiness is all that matters in life.

By establishing the idea of truth as belonging to a realm of reality outside of experience, Plato set the stage for political activity to be replaced by the activity of experts. According to Plato, we cannot trust our senses to accurately judge reality, and so if we do not want to risk being tricked by what merely appears to be true, we must instead trust the judgment of experts. Today we do this all the time. We're not sure how we feel, so we go to the doctor. We're not sure how something will taste, so we ask the waiter. We're not sure if we should watch a movie, so we read reviews. And if we're not sure if we can trust experts, then we ask Google. But if debating our judgments about reality with each other is how we become human, then replacing our judgment with the judgment of experts is to replace the political project of becoming *human* with the scientific project of becoming *certain*.

Yet against such a view it may be argued that the elevation of truth and certainty over experience and consensus has unquestionably led to advances in every scientific field, allowing us to gain innumerable insights into the nature of reality. Excluding citizens from scientific debate has without a doubt allowed scientists to work much more efficiently than would have been the case if scientists had needed the polis to reach a consensus every time they wanted to conduct an experiment. Furthermore, excluding citizens from scientific debate is not meant to be seen as having benefits only for scientists, as the ability to better understand reality allows scientists to help citizens lead better lives.

For this reason in politics too consensus has been replaced with certainty as democracy has been replaced with *bureaucracy*. Citizens no longer participate in political debates but instead participate in the act of voting to choose representatives. Representatives no longer participate in political debates but instead participate in the act of voting to choose policies. Such policies are created and managed by bureaucrats, by political experts who apply the methodologies of science to the problems of life. So scientists help citizens lead better lives because bureaucrats use the scientific understanding of reality to create for citizens the best life possible. From this perspective then it would be wrong to distinguish the political project of becoming human from the scientific project of becoming certain since certainty should be seen as necessary for the betterment of humanity. In other words, *scientific progress is human progress*.

Such an argument is certainly hard to argue against, for which reason we can see why the value of scientific progress was able to defeat competing values and become the highest value in just about every society on Earth today.

Consequently, we now take for granted that humanity has advanced alongside science, which we can see, for example, when we trace human history from the perspective of scientific history as a steady progression from the Dark Ages to the Renaissance to the Enlightenment to Modernity. And yet Arendt argues that our faith in scientific progress has led us not to truth and certainty, but to nihilism and disaster.

According to Arendt, it is not an accident that the scientific politics of bureaucracies would have led to world wars and to the creation of the atomic bomb. Political progress has been marked by the end of slavery, by the victory of suffrage movements, and by the passage of civil rights legislation. Arendt points out that such progress required that the "brute force" that kept people in servitude was moved more and more out of the domestic realm and placed instead in the political realm as bureaucrats became increasingly confident that they would be able to keep such force under control. The consolidation of brute force in the hands of the government allowed for the liberation of women and minorities from the coercive violence that historically reigned in households. But such liberation from the household did not mean that the liberated were free to become human as it did for the Ancient Greeks.

The liberated were indeed free to leave the household and enter the public realm. However, as political activities had become the activities of experts rather than of citizens, the only activity left for modern-day citizens in the modern-day agora was that of work. In other words, the freedom of the liberated was not political freedom, it was only the freedom to join the labor market. As Arendt writes,

> ... the overall development of society—at least until it reaches the point where automation truly does away with labor—is moving uniformly toward making all its members "laborers," human beings whose activity, whatever it may be, primarily serves to provide life's necessities. In this sense, too, the exclusion of brute force from the life of society has for now resulted only in leaving an incomparably larger space than ever before to the necessity life imposes on everyone. Necessity, not freedom, rules the life of society; and it is not by chance that the concept of necessity has come to dominate all modern philosophies of history, where modern thought has sought to find its philosophical orientation and self-understanding.[18]

The end of slavery and the expansion of citizenship that came with it led to a massive increase in the number of people who needed to be able to work for a living, and a massive increase in the number of products needed to be able to keep the workers alive. This in turn led to a massive increase in the productive power of the state at the same time that brute force was becoming centralized in the hands of the state. And it was this combination of the productive power that states could marshal and of the brute force that states could wield that led politics to turn from being seen as a means to freedom to being seen as a threat to freedom.

Trusting experts rather than trusting experience has enabled advances in countless scientific fields. But war is also a field capable of being advanced scientifically, as is epitomized by the creation of the atomic bomb. It is for this reason that Arendt not only questions the equating of scientific progress with human progress but questions whether there is anything truly *human* about such progress. The distrust of experience that has stretched from Platonic metaphysics to Christian theology to capitalist bureaucracy has left us incapable of judging experience for ourselves, leading us to become much less willing to try to reach consensus with each other, and much more willing (and much more able) to try to destroy each other instead.

As Arendt points out, though humans have always needed to rely on prejudices so that we could make quick judgments when we did not have time to judge experience directly, the loss of trust in judgments from experience has left us with only our prejudices to rely on. It is in the nature of prejudices as a survival instinct to make us fearful, but when prejudices become completely detached from experience, they can make us paranoid, leading us to turn our prejudices into ideologies and self-fulfilling prophecies. Consequently, our fear of the threat of politics has turned not into a quest to reinvigorate politics, but into a quest to live in a world without politics. Marx saw this quest as utopian, but Arendt warns that such a world would be "simply appalling"[19] since a world without politics would be a world without freedom.

Arendt concludes her analysis by comparing life in the modern world of bureaucratic politics—a world where politics has become something we try to evade rather than something we hope to pursue—to life in a desert. Arendt writes,

> The modern growth of worldlessness, the withering away of everything *between* us, can also be described as the spread of the desert. That we live and move in a desert-world was first recognized by Nietzsche, and it was also Nietzsche who made the first decisive mistake in diagnosing it. Like almost all who came after him, he believed that the desert is in ourselves, thereby revealing himself not only as one of the earliest conscious inhabitants of the desert but also, by the same token, as the victim of its most terrible illusion. Modern psychology is desert psychology: when we lose the faculty to judge—to suffer and condemn—we begin to think that there is something

wrong with us if we cannot live under the conditions of desert life. Insofar as psychology tries to "help" us, it helps us "adjust" to these conditions, taking away our only hope, namely that we, who are not of the desert though we live in it, are able to transform it into a human world.[20]

The purpose of this metaphor is to awaken us to precisely how lifeless our lives have become. To be in a desert is to be forced to be concerned with nothing other than bare survival, to be concerned with nothing other than the animal necessities that prevent us from experiencing human freedom.

Such is the state that Arendt believes we find ourselves in today, as our distrust of politics has led us not to distrust the scientific mind-set that has taken over politics, but instead to distrust each other. Our faith in scientific progress has culminated in our having lost faith in humanity, and precisely for this reason our faith in scientific progress has grown only stronger as it is scientific progress that is supposed to fix all that is flawed in humanity. Consequently, the more we suffer from scientific progress, the more we turn to scientific progress to cure our suffering. Like someone lost in a desert, we cling desperately to any guide who claims to know the way out, even if that guide was the one who led us into the desert in the first place.

It was the lifeless life of our desert world that Franz Kafka explored in his work—both in his work as an insurance claims investigator and in his work as a writer. Kafka's writing is filled with horrifically realistic depictions that reveal how trying to live in a bureaucratic system—a system that no one can explain or defend but that everyone follows without question—can result in our suddenly waking up to discover that unknown judges have found us guilty of an unknown crime. Or, what is much more likely, it can result in our waking up to discover that we have somehow turned into a monstrous life-form that yearns to become human, a yearning that is experienced not as hope, but as torture.

It will perhaps come as no surprise that Arendt was a fan of Kafka's. Arendt wrote several essays on the importance of Kafka's work. For example, Arendt saw Kafka's *The Trial* as a story of man who falls victim to the "bureaucratic machine." As Arendt explains, it is a machine that "is kept in motion by the lies told for the sake of necessity, with the accepted implication that a man unwilling to submit to the 'world order' of this machine is thereby considered guilty of a crime against some kind of divine order."[21]

Arendt's praise of Kafka's descriptions of desert life can help us to better understand her criticism of Nietzsche's diagnoses. According to Arendt, Nietzsche took too psychological a view of nihilism, identifying nihilism as a disease, a disease which, even if it could infect an entire culture, could still be traced back to human biology. Much like Fyodor Dostoyevsky—who Nietzsche said was "the only psychologist, incidentally, from whom I had anything to learn"[22]—Nietzsche studied nihilism by looking inward. For Nietzsche, the inability to come to terms with the limitations of having been born weak, of having been born mortal, of having been born human, can lead individuals to attempt to escape such limitations, an attempt that has resulted in the creation of philosophies, of religions, and of cultures that help individuals to escape from life itself.

Dostoyevsky's writings are filled with analyses of the rich and complex inner lives of his characters. Kafka's writings are instead filled with characters who are ciphers, with characters who do not have complete names, who do not have backstories, and who often feel like they were born yesterday. For Kafka, just as for Arendt, what matters most for understanding the modern world, the world of bureaucracy, is not the relationship between *mind and body*, but the relationship between *people and place*. What is particularly important for Arendt is how one type of place—such as the agora—can motivate people to form relationships with each other and to share a world together, and how another type of place—such as a desert—can motivate people to become incapable of forming relationships with others and to become concerned only with individual survival.

It is for this reason that Arendt is so opposed to psychology, to the view that if we suffer from trying to live in a desert, then our suffering is the result of who we are rather than of what the desert is doing to us. To learn to adapt to the desert, to be "resilient,"[23] can reduce our suffering, but Arendt warns that it is good that we are still capable of suffering, that our suffering is the canary in the coal mine, the alarm that tells us that we do not belong in the world in which we find ourselves. When this feeling of not belonging leads us to look inward, to blame ourselves, to try to fix ourselves, we become so focused on ourselves, on trying to figure out what is wrong with ourselves, that we only make the desert between ourselves and others worse. If being driven away from each other and being driven into ourselves is what creates nihilism, then individualistic responses to nihilism will never overcome nihilism but will instead only help to perpetuate nihilism.

The loss of politics, of consensus building, of coming together to share a world with each other, is for Arendt the result of the creation of nihilistic political systems. Such systems have not removed public spaces from the world, but has instead dehumanized those spaces, taking the possibility of political activity out of the public realm and leaving instead only the possibility of commercial activity, of working and of consuming. Working and consuming make us feel better because these activities help us to feel more at home in the world, in a world that is perpetuated by our working and consuming, by our caring more about being happy than about being human. But we cannot risk being satisfied with lifeless lives of inhuman happiness for, as Arendt concludes, such satisfaction is suicidal, as we find ourselves today in the "objective situation of nihilism where no-thingness and no-bodyness threaten to destroy the world."[24]

It is this situation, according to Arendt, that has led certain philosophers to ask questions like "Why is there something rather than nothing?" and "Why is there anybody rather than nobody?" Arendt argues that these questions appear nihilistic but they must instead be seen as antinihilistic. To ask these questions is to contest the view of the world that might seem most logical—"There should be nothing and nobody"—by forcing us to question what it is about the world that makes such views seem logical. In other words, what is logical, what is rational, what is normal, cannot be taken for granted, but must be questioned and challenged. And it is precisely such questioning and challenging of what is taken for granted that used to be known as *politics*. It is thus only by returning political activity to the public realm, by reclaiming public spaces as spaces for freedom, by seeking consensus rather than seeking votes, by acting as humans rather than surviving as animals, that we can begin to overcome nihilism *together* rather than continue to suicidally adapt to it *alone*.

WHAT IS THE FUTURE
OF NIHILISM?

The future is a prominent theme in Nietzsche's work. One of the earliest lectures he gave was subtitled "On the Future of Our Educational Institutions." The subtitle of *Beyond Good and Evil* announces that the book is a "prelude to a philosophy of the future." The final chapter of *Ecce Homo* is titled "Why I Am a Destiny." Nietzsche frequently declared that he was writing for the future and that his readers had not yet been born.

We may be tempted to think such declarations were due to the simple fact that, during his lifetime, almost no one bought any of his books. However, in *Beyond Good and Evil*, Nietzsche writes,

> True philosophers reach for the future with a creative hand and everything that is and was becomes a means, a tool, a hammer for them. ... It has become

increasingly clear to me that the philosopher, being *necessarily* a man of tomorrow and the day after tomorrow, has, in every age, been and has *needed* to be at odds with his today: his enemy has always been the ideals of today.[1]

To conceive of a philosophy of the future, to write for the future, is thus, according to Nietzsche, to be in opposition to the present and, in particular, to be in opposition to the "ideals" of the present. Such opposition arises because the future is viewed not only in terms of what *will* be the case but also in terms of what *should* be the case. In other words, to put forth a vision of the future is to engage in what Nietzsche calls "active nihilism."[2] Rather than sit back and let the present destroy the future ("passive nihilism"), to engage in active nihilism is to destroy the present to create the future, to destroy the destructive ideals of the present in order to create new ideals and bring about the future that we want.

The Land of the Free and the Home of the Nihilist

In the previous chapters of this book we have seen that nihilism existed in the past and that nihilism exists in the present, and so there is every reason to believe that nihilism *will* exist in the future. We have also seen a variety of arguments as to why nihilism *should not* exist in the future, arguments that all point to the danger that the more nihilistic we become, the more likely it is that we will have no future. From the Nietzschean perspective, then, the question that we need to ask is this: *What are the ideals in the present that we must oppose in order to create a future without nihilism?*

Nietzsche's answer to this question would appear to be that we must oppose the ideal of asceticism, an ideal that manifests itself morally in the value of self-sacrifice and scientifically in the value of truth. The "no" of asceticism, the "no" to life, has become the moral "no" that demands we restrain our instincts and the scientific "no" that invalidates opposing perspectives. Nietzsche, however, wanted us to say "yes" to instincts, to multiplicity, to life. It is because morality and science are two sides of the same "no" that Nietzsche argues that the ascetic ideal has no opposition. Rather than accept the commonly held view that science is the enemy of religion and is therefore the enemy of the ascetic ideal, Nietzsche instead contends that science is the latest incarnation of the ascetic ideal and is just as dependent upon faith as is religion.[3]

Arendt agreed with Nietzsche that we should challenge the ideal of truth, and the faith in science that it inspired, as such faith culminated in the death of politics and the birth of the atomic bomb. And yet, due to his opposition to the ideal of self-sacrifice, Nietzsche's active nihilism led

From the Nietzschean perspective, then, the question that we need to ask is this: *What are the ideals in the present that we must oppose in order to create a future without nihilism?*

him to promote counterideals like the Emersonian ideal of self-reliance and the Darwinian ideal of self-overcoming. As Arendt argued, such individualistic ideals can result in the very passive nihilism they are meant to counteract. Nietzsche's fear of what he saw as the "herd instinct" may have prevented him from considering that such herds arise not because of nihilistic *instincts*, but because of nihilistic *systems*, systems that can only be fought collectively and that are perpetuated when we instead try to act on our own.

For both de Beauvoir and Arendt, individualistic ideals such as self-reliance and self-overcoming are precisely what we must oppose if we are to create a future free from nihilism. For example, in her account of her time spent traveling across America in 1947, de Beauvoir writes,

> What is most striking to me, and most discouraging, is that they are so apathetic while being neither blind nor unconscious. They know and deplore the oppression of thirteen million blacks, the terrible poverty of the South, the almost equally desperate poverty that pollutes the big cities. They witness the rise, more ominous every day, of racism and reactionary attitudes—the birth of a kind of fascism. They know that their country is responsible for the world's future. But they themselves don't feel responsible for anything, because they don't think

they can do anything in this world. At the age of twenty, they are convinced that their thought is futile, their good intentions ineffective: "America is too vast and heavy a body for one individual to move it." And this evening I formulate what I've been thinking for days. In America, the individual is nothing. He is made into an abstract object of worship; by persuading him of his individual value, one stifles the awakening of a collective spirit in him. But reduced to himself in this way, he is robbed of any concrete power.[4]

De Beauvoir here makes clear that self-exaltation leads to self-destruction. America is an individualistic nation, a *ruggedly individualistic* nation, a nation where citizens are supposed to have the life and liberty necessary to pursue happiness. However, rather than happiness, what de Beauvoir found in America was a nation of individuals who had become "so apathetic while being neither blind nor unconscious." The Americans who de Beauvoir met were able to recognize that poverty, racism, and oppression in America made political change desperately necessary in order to avoid "the birth of a kind of fascism." But they felt so powerless as individuals to effect political change that they responded instead by effecting the only change they were individually powerful enough to achieve: they became *unfeeling*.

That de Beauvoir identified American apathy as a result of individuals having been "robbed of any concrete power" suggests a connection here to Arendt's argument that we must think of nihilism as political rather than as psychological. What de Beauvoir described as the powerless power of America is what Arendt described as the lifeless life of a desert. To respond to the feeling of individual powerlessness by making oneself unfeeling is to respond to the suffering of finding oneself in a desert by *adapting to the desert*.

We seek to adapt because a system that idealizes individualism and champions autonomy as the key to happiness leads individuals living in that system to feel that they *should* be happy. Any unhappiness is consequently seen as a sign that something is wrong, though not wrong with *the system*, but with *the individual*. Individualism and autonomy are thus destructive insofar as they lead us to become obsessed with personal happiness and to view our unhappiness as something that divides us from others, as something that makes us abnormal, and as something that must be cured.

Rather than discover whether others are similarly unhappy, the ideal of personal happiness motivates us to fear revealing our own unhappiness to others and to instead pretend to be happy to avoid the risk of being seen as abnormal. Such fear entails that we cannot know whether the others who seem so happy and so normal are actually

A system built on life, liberty, and the pursuit of happiness can induce nihilism by treating lifelessness, oppression, and unhappiness as *personal feelings*, as a person's pathological inability to be happy, which motivates within us the nihilistic desire to *change ourselves* rather than the political demand to *change the system*.

pretending too. And so we cannot know whether the seemingly happy herd that Nietzsche warned us to avoid may in fact be made up of individuals who are just as unhappy living in a desert as we are, and who are thus individuals we need to engage with if we are to have any hope of escaping the desert. So a system built on life, liberty, and the pursuit of happiness can induce nihilism by treating lifelessness, oppression, and unhappiness as *personal feelings*, as feelings that reveal a person's pathological inability to be happy, the result of which is that we respond to our suffering with the nihilistic desire to *change ourselves* rather than with the political demand to *change the system*.

Technology and Nihilism

If we are to create a future without nihilism by opposing individualistic ideals and the nihilism-inducing systems that champion them, then we must realize that such systems are not only political but also *technological*. Or to be more precise, we must realize that our politics is technological and that our technologies are political.

To say that politics is technological is not the same as merely saying that we engage in politics through technologies. It is of course obvious that political activities require technologies, such as when we use a paper and pencil to cast a vote or when we use Twitter to organize a protest.

But what is less obvious is how technologies can influence and even *shape* our politics, such as when we take for granted that the only options for political action available to us are the options that show up on our computer screens.

We take such things for granted because we believe that technologies do not have the power to act *independently*. To suggest that technologies do have the power to effect change on their own is to sound like you are suggesting that technologies are alive. After all, even robots only act based on their programming, on programming written by humans. Consequently, we tend to think it absurd to worry about what technologies can do to people, as what we should worry about instead is what people can do with technologies.

Such a view is what has come to be known in philosophy of technology as the *instrumental* or *neutral* view of technology. It is this view that Heidegger warned was the most dangerous possible view to take of technology precisely because it is the view that is most common. After being exiled from academia due to his collaboration with the Nazis, Heidegger tried to resurrect his career by delivering a series of public lectures in Germany during the 1950s, the most famous of which was titled "The Question Concerning Technology."

In the lecture Heidegger argues that we do not realize what technologies are doing to us because we have become too obsessed with what technologies allow us to do. We can turn rivers into electric plants, we can turn forests into newspapers, and we can even turn the Sun into a battery. Yet it is this mindset, this *framing* of nature as a means to our ends, that Heidegger sees as what is tricking us into thinking we are in control of technologies—what Heidegger refers to, echoing Nietzsche, as the "will to mastery"[5]—rather than realizing that we are being controlled by technologies. What Heidegger endeavors to show is that using technologies leads us to see the world through technologies, to think in accordance with the logic of technology.

Heidegger argues that the "essence" of technology is not its instrumentality, nor even its being technological, but rather its "way of revealing."[6] Technologies reveal the world to us in a particular way, in a way that, according to Heidegger, has changed in the modern era. Traditional technologies revealed the world to us as powerful, such as when a windmill shows the force of the wind or when a bridge shows the danger of trying to enter the water rather than cross over it. Modern technologies, however, reveal the world to us as powerful in a different sense, in the sense of the world being *full of power*, of power that we can store, that we can stockpile, and that we can use to do what we want when we want.

The logic of modern technology is characterized by Heidegger as the logic of "setting-in-order,"[7] a logic that reduces reality—*all* reality—to the logic of means and ends, the logic where everything has meaning only insofar as we can use it *in order to* get something we want. We are of course aware of the pervasiveness of this logic, but we mistakenly assume that the ends of our activities are determined solely by us, solely by humans. So we assume that if we find ourselves in a technological world thinking instrumentally, it is only because we are using technologies as instruments, as *our* means to *our* ends.

However, what Heidegger points out is that if these ends are ours, it is not because we chose them, but because we have come to identify with them. When in an airport we instinctively look for a seat near an electrical outlet, we think we're just looking for the best seat. But really we're sitting in accordance with what is "best" for our phone, and for our laptop, and for whatever other devices we now unquestionably think it is "best" for us to have when we travel. In other words, not only do technologies shape how we see the world and how we act in the world but they also shape how we evaluate the world, how we determine what is "best" and what is "worst."

Technologies have enabled us to feel more and more powerful, but only because we do not realize that in reducing reality to the logic of means and ends, we are ourselves becoming more and more reduced by this logic. When we seek out an outlet in order to plug in a device, we do not realize that we have ourselves become a means to an end, a means to the end of the device. In such a situation the device has turned us into an instrument of its ends. What is best *for the device* becomes what is best *for us*.

Devices frequently require that we organize our activities in accordance with what is necessary to keep them functioning properly. We are even becoming increasingly interrupted in our activities in order to help the device carry out functions. These are functions that often we did not choose for the device to perform, functions that we do not even understand. The device informs us that we need to download an update, and we click download. The device informs us that we need to click accept, and we click accept. The device informs us that we need to restart the device, and we click restart. The device informs us that we need to create a new password, so we enter a password— only the device then informs us that it does not accept our password, and it advises us on how to enter the *best* password, so we keep trying until we meet the device's approval.

In other words, technologies are powerful; we are not. We only feel powerful to the extent that we align our ends with the ends of our technologies so that when we act in order to serve our technologies, we feel like we are acting in order to serve ourselves. But what is important for Heidegger is that whether we are acting in order to serve technologies or in order to serve ourselves, we are still acting only in accordance with the logic of *setting-in-order*.

To live in accordance with such a logic is to have become dehumanized.

According to Heidegger, in reducing nature to a power source that can be called upon on demand, technologies have at the same time reduced humanity to a power source that can be called upon on demand. Making clear the connection between technology and nihilism, Heidegger warns, "Nihilism is the world-historical movement of the peoples of the earth who have been drawn into the power realm of the modern age," for which reason "those who fancy themselves free of nihilism perhaps push forward its development most fundamentally."[8] We say that technologies are empowering us, but that is because we have elevated technologies under the guise that in so doing we have elevated ourselves. We take for granted that we live in a "technological world," and in order to maintain the illusion of empowerment, the illusion that this world is *for us*, we have redefined ourselves as "technological beings,"[9] as "technomoral creatures,"[10] and as "informationally embodied organisms (*inforgs*)."[11] Technologies therefore not only shape how we think, how we act, and how we value, but also redefine what it means to be human.

The French sociologist and theologian Jacques Ellul similarly warned that the illusion that we are in control of our technologies blinds us to how much technologies have come to control us. In his 1977 book *The Technological*

System, Ellul warns that technologies not only influence us individually but also influence us politically. As Ellul argues, against the "simple view" that "the state decides, technology obeys," we instead "have to ask who in the state intervenes, and how the state intervenes, i.e., how a decision is reached and by whom in reality not in the idealist vision."[12]

Ellul points out that we cannot make decisions about technologies if we do not understand how they work. Lawmakers therefore are increasingly forced to turn to technology experts in order to make laws about technologies. But as laws about technologies would necessarily impact those very same technology experts, Ellul calls into question the possibility that technology experts could provide their expertise objectively, as any risk to technologies would be a risk to themselves.

It should come as no surprise therefore that political decisions rarely, if ever, come into conflict with technological progress. Consequently, companies like Facebook and Google can act in ways that endanger not only individual users, but entire societies. And yet tech companies neither fear the wrath of those users nor of those societies, for users now depend on tech companies much more than tech companies depend on users. Facebook and Google can abuse us—such as by violating our privacy—because, like abusers, they know we have nowhere else to go. Facebook and Google respond to allegations of abuse by essentially daring us to leave them, as they know that we'll always end up coming back for more.

Yet, as Heidegger helps us to see, the true danger posed by companies like Facebook and Google is not that they *violate* our privacy, but that they *redefine* what we think "privacy" means. Facebook and Google—not to mention tech companies like Apple, Amazon, Tinder, and Twitter— all defend their privacy-endangering practices by simply pointing out that they are only giving users what users want. If users want to be social, then apps and devices need to be able to help them find others to be social with, and need to be able to find more and more ways for users to share more and more of their lives with others. And if users want to meet the *right* others, and learn about the *right* events, and find the *right* products, then apps and devices need to know as much as possible about the activities and interests of users.

Apps and devices study users, treating users as not only sources of power but as sources of information. Technologies have always required power in order to function, but apps and devices increasingly require information in order to function. But when we are motivated by our technologies to share more and more of our private lives with technologies and through technologies, we do not feel reduced by technologies to means to *their* ends, as instead we come to view the end of sharing as having always been *our* end. Consequently, it is only the dramatic abuses of users' trust, only when tech companies are found to have been selling users' information without permission, or when a data breach is found to have made users' information public, that lead users to feel outraged. For users are motivated to see the abuses of trust that tech companies perform everyday not as *violations* but as simply the price that must be paid for *wanting to be social.*

Traditional definitions of privacy have thus come to be seen as outdated, and people who still want to live in accordance with a more traditional sense of privacy have come to be seen as *antisocial*. To be seen as antisocial, in a world where being social has become the norm, is to be seen as *abnormal*. Tech companies justify their practices by claiming that they are giving users what users want, but in a technological world, in a world where people can be ostracized for not being sufficiently technological, it is increasingly difficult to distinguish whether what users want is determined more by *desire* or by *fear*.

Though of course, from the perspective of Heidegger and of Ellul, technologies shape both our desires and our fears, and so tech companies cannot justify their practices by referring to what users want since what users want is shaped by those practices. The ubiquity of technologies has made it impossible for us to take a perspective on technologies that is free from the influence of technologies. But if we cannot be free from the influence of technologies, then we cannot make independent judgments about technologies. And if we live in a technological world, then this means that we cannot make independent judgments about the world in which we live. So technological progress makes us feel more and more powerful, and yet this progress is making us politically more and more powerless.

From a Nietzschean perspective we find ourselves in a technological world because our nihilistic need to avoid feeling alone, to avoid feeling powerless, and to avoid feeling feelings leads us to seek out new ways to avoid feeling *human*. We have then moved from escaping reality by using the imagination to enter worlds like Heaven and Hell to instead escaping reality by using movies and consoles to enter worlds like Hogwarts and Hyrule. From an Arendtian perspective, however, we find ourselves in a technological world not because humans are nihilistic and are constantly seeking new forms of escape, but because political systems that promise individual happiness and produce individual suffering lead us to feel that we are individually to blame for our suffering. And so we have moved from seeking psychological cures like pills and therapy to help us to adapt to the lifeless life of a desert to seeking technological cures like Netflix and Fitbit to help us to adapt to the lifeless life of a technological world.

In other words, for both Nietzsche and Arendt there would be no question as to whether technological progress has furthered or hindered the progress of nihilism. Instead the only question would be how we came to equate technological progress with human progress, and how we can prevent this equation from continuing to blind us to the nihilistic nature of technological progress.

Fighting Nihilism with Nihilism

If we are seeking a way to be able to destroy the life-denying values of the past and present so that we can create a future based on new life-affirming values, then technologies would seem to have the destructive and creative potential necessary to achieve such aims. Yet rather than produce active nihilism, in the previous section we saw that technologies are primarily producing passive nihilism. Ironically, the problem seems to be that technologies are not as "disruptive" as tech companies claim them to be.

As Heidegger and Ellul showed, technologies are certainly dangerous, but their danger has come not in the form of destroying values, but in the form of redefining our values. Technological progress has created a technological world, but this new world still has old values, and so if we want to create a future based on new values, and if we cannot imagine a future that is not technological, then either we need to change what we imagine to be possible, or we need to change the nature of technological progress.

From the perspective of ethics and politics, technological progress has not been revolutionary, it has been overwhelmingly *conservative*. Technologies are increasingly interfering with our ability to lead autonomous lives, to be able to think rationally, to be able to make decisions based on what we know to be true rather than merely on what is presented to us as true. And yet the tech companies that create these technologies are not justifying their interference by promoting new values, by trying to replace the humanistic values of autonomy, of rationality, and of truth that go back at least as far as the Enlightenment. Instead tech companies deny that any interference is intentional and argue that what is seen by critics as intentional interference is merely their attempt to develop tools that could be used to uphold humanistic values by helping us to become more autonomous, more rational, and more aware of the truth.

On April 10, 2018, Facebook CEO Mark Zuckerberg was called to testify before Congress about the role Facebook played in scandals surrounding interference in the 2016 U.S. presidential election. Zuckerberg did not defend Facebook's role in the scandals by questioning the value of democracy, but instead defended Facebook as a tool in the service of democracy. Zuckerberg admitted that, as a tool, Facebook could be misused, and so he pledged to develop new tools—such as algorithms that could detect and delete "fake news"—to ensure that Facebook's "tools are used for good."[13]

Zuckerberg did not feel the need to define what he meant by "good," however. This omission points toward a desire to take traditional values for granted rather than create new values. Facebook may have helped to destroy our traditional means for engaging in democracy—as candidates now hold virtual town halls and citizens now debate each other with memes rather than with meetings—but traditional values like the value of engaging in democracy have nevertheless remained intact. Indeed Facebook has gotten in so much trouble politically largely because it provides so many new means for engaging in democracy.

As Ellul foresaw, democratic states are being transformed into technological states. But Ellul was careful to point out that such a transformation does not mean that the tech experts, or "technicians," creating these transformations have any interest in creating new values, in creating a *technocracy*. Ellul writes,

> Does that imply the emergence of a technocracy?
> Absolutely not in the sense of a political power
> directly exercised by technicians, and not in the
> sense of the technicians' desire to exercise power.
> The latter aspect is practically without interest.
> There are very few technicians who wish to have
> political power. As for the former aspect it is still
> part of a traditional analysis of the state: people see a

technician sitting in the government minister's chair. But under the influence of technology, it is the entire state that is modified. One can say that there will soon be no more (and indeed less and less) political power (with all its contents: ideology, authority, the power of man over man, etc.). We are watching the birth of a technological state, which is anything but a technocracy; this new state has chiefly technological functions, a technological organization, and a rationalized system of decision-making.[14]

As Ellul points out, we must not assume that just because technicians like Zuckerberg wield the power necessary to create technological states that they want to use that power to achieve any purposes that are ethical or political as opposed to merely economic. Technological states are seen by Ellul as merely technologically enhanced bureaucracies rather than as technocracies because the technicians who could rule have no interest in ruling. So technicians help to create states that are essentially apolitical, states that are focused solely on maintaining the status quo, on keeping the ends of the state constant while what changes is only the means available to achieve those ends.

Arendt described the rise of bureaucracy as the rise of "no-man rule."[15] In a bureaucracy decisions are made by determining scientifically what is best for society, what is best not for anyone in particular, but for the "everyman," for the statistically average human who is meant to represent *everyone* because he is *no one*. Similarly, a theme that runs through the work of the French philosopher Michel Foucault is that, in a society governed by statistical modeling and scientific reasoning, humans are reduced to the behaviors and characteristics that can be identified as distributively common or "normal." Consequently, what is found to be uncommon and uncharacteristic is viewed as "abnormal," as statistical anomalies to be *removed*, whether by educational, legal, or medical means.

This method of decision-making is powerful because it creates an almost impenetrable aura of *objectivity*. Scientific reasoning allows bureaucrats to wave away accusations of bias and prejudice by simply arguing that numbers have no biases and math has no prejudices. Statistical argumentation even allows racism and sexism to seem like the product of *natural* superiority rather than the product of *political* superiority. However, so long as the statistical modeling and scientific reasoning is performed by humans, critics will always be able to counter the claims of bureaucrats by pointing out that measurements might be unbiased, but the humans determining what is to be measured and how are not.

The technological state described by Ellul is thus not the *destruction* of the bureaucratic state, but its *perfection*. If citizens want to live in a state free from the corrupting influence of self-interested bureaucrats, then a state governed by machines will be seen as far more trustworthy than a state governed by humans. For this reason "smart city"[16] projects have become increasingly popular. Governance by nonhuman bureaucrats—otherwise known as algorithms—can make citizens feel safe from bias and prejudice and can make political leaders feel safe from being *accused* of being biased and prejudiced.

And so, in a technological state, no-man rule can become quite literal. Statistical modeling performed by algorithms can reduce humans to data sets, and the scientific reasoning that leads us to trust algorithms can reduce politics to cost-benefit analysis. But again, what is important to realize here is that this reductive treatment of humans and of politics is not a new technological project; it is merely the culmination of the project of the Enlightenment, of the project to create a science of humanity. Hence, even the value we ascribe to something as futuristic as artificial intelligence should be seen not as a new value, but as a very old value in shiny new packaging.

Yet it is precisely because technological progress is not as truly revolutionary as tech entrepreneurs claim that technologies can nevertheless help us to combat nihilism. As Heidegger argued, the essence of technology is revealing. If technologies are not helping to create new values but are instead operating in accordance with old values, then the nihilism created by technologies can help

Governance by nonhuman bureaucrats—otherwise known as algorithms—can make citizens feel safe from bias and prejudice and can make political leaders feel safe from being accused of being biased and prejudiced.

to reveal to us the nihilistic nature of these values. We live in a technological world, in a world that is the realization of the dreams of the Enlightenment. To find this world becoming more and more nihilistic is to see revealed that these dreams are actually nightmares, nightmares from which we need to wake up before it's too late.

Technologies may not be creating new values, but they are creating new forms of nihilism.[17] As Nietzsche suggested, it is possible that we could become so nihilistic, that we could become so destructive, that we could destroy even our nihilistic values and the nihilistic systems that sustain them. So to end on a hopeful note, if the nihilism generated by technological progress doesn't make us too self-destructive, then perhaps instead it will make us just destructive enough to force us to finally become creative. In other words, if nihilism doesn't kill us, it might make us stronger.

GLOSSARY

Absurdity
Concept used by existential philosophers to highlight that to be human is to be condemned to seek meaning in what is meaningless, to seek order in what is chaotic.

Authenticity
Concept used by existential philosophers to indicate a way of being in the world that confronts what it means to be human.

Autonomy
From *auto* ("self") and *nomos* ("law"), typically understood to mean "self-legislating," but can have very different meanings depending on whether "self" is understood to be only the rational self (as in Kant) or the desiring self (as in everyday usage).

Determinism
Philosophical position that holds that the actions of an individual are caused by someone or something other than that individual.

Dualism
Philosophical position that holds that reality is actually composed of two separate realities, most often associated with mind/body dualism, or the division of mental reality from physical reality.

Epistemology
Area of philosophy that deals with questions about what is and is not knowable (e.g., What is knowledge? What is the difference between facts and opinions?).

Ethics
Area of philosophy that deals with questions about how humans should and should not live (e.g., What is the good life? Should we act on the basis of principles or of likely consequences?).

Existentialism
Philosophical theory that is primarily focused on what it means to be human and, in particular, on what it means to live as finite creatures who are capable of knowing that we are finite creatures.

Freedom
Concept that is typically used to mean that humans are not determined in some way, such as ethically (e.g., to be autonomous rather than heteronomous) or politically (e.g., to be a citizen rather than a slave).

Humanism
Philosophical theory that can be traced back to the Enlightenment, focused on the promotion of human-centric values (e.g., autonomy) as opposed to religious values (e.g., faith).

Inauthenticity
Concept used by existential philosophers to indicate a way of being in the world that rejects or evades what it means to be human.

Metaphysics
Area of philosophy that deals with questions about the ultimate foundations of experiential reality (e.g., Why is there something rather than nothing? What is the being of beings?).

Nihilism
Wanting complicated ideas reduced to one sentence made easily available in the back of a book.

Positivism
Philosophical theory that holds that reality is objectively knowable through the scientific method of verificationism (i.e., factual claims can be verified through observation and claims that cannot be so verified are not factual).

Postmodernism
Term often used more to denigrate philosophical positions rather than to promote them, but as a philosophical position it is often used to refer to the view that meanings are not objective facts but are social constructions.

Relativism
Philosophical position that holds that anything taken to be true is true only for the person who believes it; for example, moral relativism holds that moral values have different meanings for different people and so have no universal meaning applicable for all people for all time that would justify one group of people with one set of values judging the morality of a different group of people with a different set of values.

Scientism
The belief that science can and should solve all problems, which, when taken to the extreme, becomes a religious faith in science that, hypocritically, rejects all traditionally recognized religious faiths as unscientific.

Transcendence
To go beyond experience, which implies that there exists a realm of reality beyond experience.

NOTES

Chapter 1

1. Vernon Parrington, *The Beginnings of Critical Realism in America* (London: Routledge, 2017), 146.

2. "Wendell Phillips Justifies Nihilism," *Los Angeles Herald*, July 28, 1881, 3. Available online: https://cdnc.ucr.edu/cgi-bin/cdnc?a=d&d=LAH18810728.2.20&dliv=none&e=-------en--20--1--txt-txIN-------1.

3. Jerry Seinfeld, "Show #1575," *Late Show with David Letterman*, CBS Network, March 21, 2001.

Chapter 2

1. Plato, *Republic*, trans. G. M. A. Grube (Indianapolis: Hackett, 1992), 187.

2. Plato, *Five Dialogues: Euthyphro, Apology, Crito, Meno, Phaedo*, trans. G. M. A. Grube (Indianapolis: Hackett, 2002), 41.

3. René Descartes, *Meditations on First Philosophy*, trans. John Cottingham (Cambridge: Cambridge University Press, 1986), 19.

4. David Hume, *A Treatise of Human Nature*, ed. David Fate Norton and Mary J. Norton (Oxford: Oxford University Press, 2000), 72.

5. Hume, *Treatise*, 175.

6. Immanuel Kant, *Critique of Pure Reason*, trans. Norman Kemp Smith (Basingstoke: Palgrave Macmillan, 1929), 72.

7. Michael Allen Gillespie, *Nihilism before Nietzsche* (Chicago: University of Chicago Press, 1995), 65.

8. Robert E. Helbling, *The Major Works of Heinrich von Kleist* (New York: New Directions, 1975), 24.

9. Friedrich Nietzsche, "Twilight of the Idols," in *The Portable Nietzsche*, ed. Walter Kaufmann (New York: Viking Penguin, 1954), 467.

10. https://www.britannica.com/biography/Elisabeth-Forster-Nietzsche.

11. Friedrich Nietzsche, *The Will to Power*, trans. Walter Kaufmann and R. J. Hollingdale (New York: Vintage Books, 1967), 7. Note is dated from 1885–1886.

12. Nietzsche, *Will to Power*, 9. Note is dated from Spring–Fall 1887.

13. Nietzsche, *Will to Power*, 14. Note is dated from Spring–Fall 1887.

14. Nietzsche, *Will to Power*, 17. Note is dated from Spring–Fall 1887.

15. Nietzsche, *Will to Power*, 23. Note is dated from November 1887–March 1888.

16. Friedrich Nietzsche, *On the Genealogy of Morals and Ecce Homo*, trans. Walter Kaufmann (New York: Vintage Books, 1989), 17.

17. Nietzsche, *Genealogy*, 38.

18. Nietzsche, *Genealogy*, 42.

19. Nietzsche, *Genealogy*, 35.

20. Nietzsche, *Genealogy*, 62.

21. Nietzsche, *Genealogy*, 97.

22. Nietzsche, *Genealogy*, 79.

23. Friedrich Nietzsche, *The Gay Science*, trans. Walter Kaufmann (New York: Random House, 1974), 181–182.

24. Nietzsche, *Will to Power*, 9.

25. For a more detailed discussion of these methods, see Nolen Gertz, *Nihilism and Technology* (London: Rowman & Littlefield International, 2018).

Chapter 3

1. Woody Allen, *Four Films of Woody Allen* (New York: Random House, 1982), 64.

2. http://daria.wikia.com/wiki/Daria_Morgendorffer.

3. Glenn Eichler, "The Misery Chick," *Daria*, MTV, July 21, 1997.

4. Nietzsche, *Genealogy*, 19.

Chapter 4

1. See, for example, Julian Baggini, *What's It All About? Philosophy and the Meaning of Life* (London: Granta Books, 2004).

2. See, for example, Arthur Schopenhauer, *The World as Will and Representation: Volume 1*, trans. Christopher Janaway (Cambridge: Cambridge University Press, 2010).

3. Donald Crosby, *The Specter of the Absurd: Sources & Criticisms of Modern Nihilism* (Albany: State University of New York Press, 1988), 35.

4. James Tartaglia, *Philosophy in a Meaningless Life: A System of Nihilism, Consciousness and Reality* (London: Bloomsbury Academic, 2016), 38.

5. Tartaglia, *Philosophy in a Meaningless Life*, 44.

6. Jean-Paul Sartre, *Being and Nothingness*, trans. Hazel Barnes (New York: Washington Square Press, 1992), 725. See also Jean-Paul Sartre, "The Humanism of Existentialism," in Jean-Paul Sartre, *Essays in Existentialism*, ed. Wade Baskin (New York: Citadel Press, 1965), 34.

7. Simone de Beauvoir, *The Second Sex*, trans. Constance Borde and Sheila Malovany-Chevallier (New York: Vintage Books, 2009), 283.

8. Jean-François Lyotard, *The Postmodern Condition: A Report on Knowledge*, trans. Geoff Bennington and Brian Massumi (Manchester: Manchester University Press, 1984), xxiii.

9. Lyotard, *The Postmodern Condition*, xxiv.

10. Simone de Beauvoir, *The Ethics of Ambiguity*, trans. Bernard Frechtman (New York: Citadel Press, 1948), 35ff.

11. De Beauvoir, *The Ethics of Ambiguity*, 52–53.

12. Søren Kierkegaard, *The Present Age*, trans. Alexander Dru (New York: Harper & Row, 1962), 34.

13. Hannah Arendt, *The Life of the Mind* (San Diego: Harcourt, 1978), 176.

Chapter 5

1. Günther Anders, "The World as Phantom and as Matrix," *Dissent* 3:1 (Winter 1956), 14.

2. Theodor Adorno, "How to Look at Television," in *The Culture Industry*, ed. J. M. Bernstein (London: Routledge Classics, 2001), 158–177.

3. Paulo Freire, *Pedagogy of the Oppressed*, trans. Myra Bergman Ramos (New York: Continuum International, 1970), 71.

4. Freire, *Pedagogy*, 73–74.

5. Karl Marx, "From the First Manuscript: 'Alienated Labour,'" in *The Portable Karl Marx*, ed. Eugene Kamenka (New York: Viking Penguin, 1983), 133.

6. Marx, "Alienated Labour," 136.

7. Marx, "Alienated Labour," 137.

8. Plato, *Republic*, 257.

9. Marx, "Alienated Labour," 142.

10. Hannah Arendt, "Introduction *into* Politics," in Hannah Arendt, *The Promise of Politics*, ed. Jerome Kohn (New York: Schocken Books, 2005), 108.

11. Arendt, "Introduction," 117.

12. Arendt, "Introduction," 128–129.

13. Aristotle, *Nicomachean Ethics*, ed. Roger Crisp (Cambridge: Cambridge University Press, 2000), 11.

14. Arendt, "Introduction," 132–133.

15. Plato, *Republic*, 107.

16. Plato, *Republic*, 91.

17. Plato, *Republic*, 35–36.

18. Arendt, "Introduction," 149.

19. Arendt, "Introduction," 153.

20. Arendt, "Introduction," 201.

21. Hannah Arendt, "Franz Kafka, Appreciated Anew," in Hannah Arendt, *Reflections on Literature and Culture*, ed. Susannah Young-ah Gottlieb (Stanford: Stanford University Press, 2007), 96.

22. Friedrich Nietzsche, *Twilight of the Idols*, trans. Duncan Large (Oxford: Oxford University Press, 1998), 70.

23. See Robin James, *Resilience & Melancholy: Pop Music, Feminism, Neoliberalism* (Winchester: Zero Books, 2015), 6–8.

24. Arendt, "Introduction," 204.

Chapter 6

1. Friedrich Nietzsche, *Beyond Good and Evil*, ed. Rolf-Peter Horstmann and Judith Norman (Cambridge: Cambridge University Press, 2002), 106.

2. Nietzsche, *Will to Power*, 17.

3. Nietzsche, *Genealogy*, 148–156. See also Babette Babich, *Nietzsche's Philosophy of Science: Reflecting Science on the Ground of Art and Life* (Albany: State University of New York Press, 1994).

4. Simone de Beauvoir, *America Day by Day*, trans. Carol Cosman (Berkeley: University of California Press, 1999), 94.

5. Martin Heidegger, "The Question Concerning Technology," in *The Question Concerning Technology and Other Essays*, trans. William Lovitt (New York: Harper & Row, 1977), 5.

6. Heidegger, "The Question Concerning Technology," 12.

7. Heidegger, "The Question Concerning Technology," 15.

8. Martin Heidegger, "The Word of Nietzsche: 'God Is Dead,'" in *The Question Concerning Technology and Other Essays*, trans. William Lovitt (New York: Harper & Row, 1977), 63.

9. Peter-Paul Verbeek, *Moralizing Technology* (Chicago: University of Chicago Press, 2011), 4.

10. Shannon Vallor, "Moral Deskilling and Upskilling in a New Machine Age: Reflections on the Ambiguous Future of Character," *Philosophy of Technology* 28, no. 1 (2015), 118.

11. Luciano Floridi, *The Ethics of Information* (Oxford: Oxford University Press, 2013), 14.

12. Jacques Ellul, *The Technological System*, trans. Joachim Neugroschel (New York: Continuum, 1980), 130.

13. Issie Lapowsky, "If Congress Doesn't Understand Facebook, What Hope Do Its Users Have?," *Wired*, April 10, 2018, https://www.wired.com/story/mark-zuckerberg-congress-day-one. See also Nolen Gertz, "Is Facebook Just

a 'Tool'?," *CIPS Blog*, April 14, 2018, http://www.cips-cepi.ca/2018/04/14/is-facebook-just-a-tool.

14. Ellul, *The Technological System*, 59.

15. Hannah Arendt, *The Human Condition* (Chicago: University of Chicago Press, 1958), 40.

16. See, for example, https://amsterdamsmartcity.com.

17. See Gertz, *Nihilism and Technology*.

BIBLIOGRAPHY

Adorno, Theodor. "How to Look at Television." In *The Culture Industry*, ed. J. M. Bernstein, London: Routledge Classics, 2001.

Allen, Woody. *Four Films of Woody Allen*. New York: Random House, 1982.

Anders, Günther. "The World as Phantom and as Matrix." *Dissent* 3:1 (Winter 1956): 14–24.

Arendt, Hannah. "Franz Kafka, Appreciated Anew." In *Reflections on Literature and Culture*, edited by Susannah Young-ah Gottlieb. Stanford: Stanford University Press, 2007.

Arendt, Hannah. *The Human Condition*. Chicago: University of Chicago Press, 1958.

Arendt, Hannah. "Introduction *into* Politics." In *The Promise of Politics*, edited by Jerome Kohn. New York: Schocken Books, 2005.

Arendt, Hannah. *The Life of the Mind*. San Diego: Harcourt, 1978.

Aristotle. *Nicomachean Ethics*. Edited by Roger Crisp. Cambridge: Cambridge University Press, 2000.

Babich, Babette. *Nietzsche's Philosophy of Science: Reflecting Science on the Ground of Art and Life*. Albany: State University of New York Press, 1994.

Baggini, Julian. *What's It All About? Philosophy and the Meaning of Life*. London: Granta Books, 2004.

Beauvoir, Simone de. *America Day by Day*. Translated by Carol Cosman. Berkeley: University of California Press, 1999.

Beauvoir, Simone de. *The Ethics of Ambiguity*. Translated by Bernard Frechtman. New York: Citadel Press, 1948.

Beauvoir, Simone de. *The Second Sex*. Translated by Constance Borde and Sheila Malovany-Chevallier. New York: Vintage Books, 2009.

Byron, George G. *Selected Poetry of Lord Byron*. Edited by Leslie A. Marchand. New York: The Modern Library, 2001.

Crosby, Donald. *The Specter of the Absurd: Sources & Criticisms of Modern Nihilism*. Albany: State University of New York Press, 1988.

Descartes, René. *Meditations on First Philosophy*. Translated by John Cottingham. Cambridge: Cambridge University Press, 1986.

Eichler, Glenn. "The Misery Chick." *Daria*. MTV. July 21, 1997.

Ellul, Jacques. *The Technological System*. Translated by Joachim Neugroschel. New York: Continuum, 1980.

Floridi, Luciano. *The Ethics of Information*. Oxford: Oxford University Press, 2013.

Foucault, Michel. *Discipline and Punish*. Translated by Alan Sheridan. New York: Vintage Books, 1995.

Freire, Paulo. *Pedagogy of the Oppressed*. Translated by Myra Bergman Ramos. New York: Continuum International, 1970.

Gertz, Nolen. "Is Facebook Just a 'Tool'?" *CIPS Blog*, April 14, 2018, http://www.cips-cepi.ca/2018/04/14/is-facebook-just-a-tool.

Gertz, Nolen. *Nihilism and Technology*. London: Rowman & Littlefield International, 2018.

Goethe, Johann Wolfgang von. *Faust: A Tragedy*. Translated by Martin Greenberg. New Haven: Yale University Press, 2014.

Gillespie, Michael Allen. *Nihilism before Nietzsche*. Chicago: University of Chicago Press, 1995.

Heidegger, Martin. *Being and Time*. Translated by John Macquarrie and Edward Robinson. New York: Harper and Row, 1962.

Heidegger, Martin. "The Question Concerning Technology." In *The Question Concerning Technology and Other Essays*, translated by William Lovitt. New York: Harper & Row, 1977.

Heidegger, Martin. "The Word of Nietzsche: 'God Is Dead.'" In *The Question Concerning Technology and Other Essays*, translated by William Lovitt. New York: Harper & Row, 1977.

Helbling, Robert E. *The Major Works of Heinrich von Kleist*. New York: New Directions, 1975.

Hume, David. *A Treatise of Human Nature*. Edited by David Fate Norton and Mary J. Norton. Oxford: Oxford University Press, 2000.

James, Robin. *Resilience & Melancholy: Pop Music, Feminism, Neoliberalism*. Winchester: Zero Books, 2015.

Kant, Immanuel. *Critique of Pure Reason*. Translated by Norman Kemp Smith. Basingstoke: Palgrave Macmillan, 1929.

Kierkegaard, Søren. *The Concept of Anxiety*. Translated by Reidar Thomte. Princeton: Princeton University Press, 1980.

Kierkegaard, Søren. *Fear and Trembling and The Sickness unto Death*. Translated by Walter Lowrie. Princeton: Princeton University Press, 2013.

Kierkegaard, Søren. *The Present Age*. Translated by Alexander Dru. New York: Harper & Row, 1962.

Lapowsky, Issie. "If Congress Doesn't Understand Facebook, What Hope Do Its Users Have?" *Wired*, April 10, 2018, https://www.wired.com/story/mark-zuckerberg-congress-day-one.

Lyotard, Jean-François. *The Postmodern Condition: A Report on Knowledge*. Translated by Geoff Bennington and Brian Massumi. Manchester: Manchester University Press, 1984.

Marx, Karl. "From the First Manuscript: 'Alienated Labour.'" In *The Portable Karl Marx*, edited by Eugene Kamenka. New York: Viking Penguin, 1983.

Nietzsche, Friedrich. *Anti-Education: On the Future of Our Educational Institutions*. Translated by Damion Searls. New York: NYRB Classics, 2015.

Nietzsche, Friedrich. *Beyond Good and Evil*. Edited by Rolf-Peter Horstmann and Judith Norman. Cambridge: Cambridge University Press, 2002.

Nietzsche, Friedrich. *The Gay Science*. Translated by Walter Kaufmann. New York: Random House, 1974.

Nietzsche, Friedrich. *On the Genealogy of Morals and Ecce Homo*. Translated by Walter Kaufmann. New York: Vintage Books, 1989.

Nietzsche, Friedrich. "Twilight of the Idols." In *The Portable Nietzsche*, edited by Walter Kaufmann. New York: Viking Penguin, 1954.

Nietzsche, Friedrich. *Twilight of the Idols*. Translated by Duncan Large. Oxford: Oxford University Press, 1998.

Nietzsche, Friedrich. *The Will to Power*. Translated by Walter Kaufmann and R. J. Hollingdale. New York: Vintage Books, 1967.

Parrington, Vernon. *The Beginnings of Critical Realism in America*. London: Routledge, 2017.

Pascal, Blaise. *Pensées*. Translated by A. J. Krailsheimer. London, Penguin Books, 1995.

Plato. *Five Dialogues: Euthyphro, Apology, Crito, Meno, Phaedo*. Translated by G. M. A. Grube. Indianapolis: Hackett, 2002.

Plato. *Republic*. Translated by G. M. A. Grube. Indianapolis: Hackett, 1992.

Sartre, Jean-Paul. *Being and Nothingness*. Translated by Hazel Barnes. New York: Washington Square Press, 1992.

Sartre, Jean-Paul. "The Humanism of Existentialism." In *Essays in Existentialism*, edited by Wade Baskin. New York: Citadel Press, 1965.

Schopenhauer, Arthur. *The World as Will and Representation: Volume 1*. Translated by Christopher Janaway. Cambridge: Cambridge University Press, 2010.

Seinfeld, Jerry. "Show #1575." *Late Show with David Letterman*. CBS Network. March 21, 2001.

Tartaglia, James. *Philosophy in a Meaningless Life: A System of Nihilism, Consciousness and Reality*. London: Bloomsbury Academic, 2016.

Turgenev, Ivan. *Fathers and Sons*. Translated by Richard Freeborn. Oxford: Oxford University Press, 2008.

Vallor, Shannon. "Moral Deskilling and Upskilling in a New Machine Age: Reflections on the Ambiguous Future of Character." *Philosophy of Technology* 28, no. 1 (2015): 107–124.

Verbeek, Peter-Paul. *Moralizing Technology*. Chicago: University of Chicago Press, 2011.

"Wendell Phillips Justifies Nihilism." *Los Angeles Herald*. July 28, 1881. Page 3. Available online: https://cdnc.ucr.edu/cgi-bin/cdnc?a=d&d=LAH18810728.2 .20&dliv=none&e=-------en--20--1--txt-txIN--------1.

Wittgenstein, Ludwig. *Philosophical Investigations*. Translated by G. E. M. Anscombe, P. M. S. Hacker, and Joachim Schulte. Oxford: Blackwell Publishing, 2009.

FURTHER READING

Adorno, Theodor. *The Culture Industry*. Edited by J. M. Bernstein. London: Routledge Classics, 2001.

Babich, Babette. "*Ex aliquo nihil*: Nietzsche on Science, Anarchy, and Democratic Nihilism." *American Catholic Philosophical Quarterly* 84, no. 2 (2010): 231–256.

der Borg, Meerten, B. "The Problem of Nihilism: A Sociological Approach." *Sociological Analysis* 49, no. 1 (1988): 1–16.

Camus, Albert. *The Myth of Sisyphus and Other Essays*. Translated by Justin O'Brien. New York: Vintage International, 1991.

Deleuze, Gilles. *Nietzsche & Philosophy*. Translated by Hugh Tomlinson. New York: Columbia University Press, 1983.

Diken, Bülent. *Nihilism*. London: Routledge, 2008.

Dostoevsky, Fyodor. *Demons: A Novel in Three Parts*. Translated by Richard Pevear and Larissa Volokhonsky. New York: Vintage Books, 1994.

Heidegger, Martin. *The Question Concerning Technology and Other Essays*. Translated by William Lovitt. New York: Harper & Row, 1977.

Kafka, Franz. *The Trial*. Translated by Breon Mitchell. New York: Shocken Books, 1998.

Lebovic, Nitzan, and Roy Ben-Shai, eds. *The Politics of Nihilism: From the Nineteenth Century to Contemporary Israel*. New York: Bloomsbury Academic, 2014.

Löwith, Karl. "The Historical Background of European Nihilism." In *Nature, History and Existentialism: And Other Critical Essays in the Philosophy of History*, edited by Arnold Levison. Evanston: Northwestern University Press, 1966.

Pearson, Keith Ansell, and Diane Morgan, eds. *Nihilism Now! Monsters of Energy*. New York: Saint Martin's Press, 2000.

Rauschning, Hermann. *Revolution of Nihilism: Warning to the West*. Translated by E. W. Dickes. New York: Longmans, Green, 1939.

Warren, Calvin. "Black Nihilism & the Politics of Hope." *The New Centennial Review* 15, no. 1 (Spring 2015): 215–248.

Weil, Simone. *Gravity and Grace*. Translated by Emma Crawford and Mario van der Ruhr. London: Routledge Classics, 2002.

Weil, Simone. *The Need for Roots*. Translated by Arthur Wills. London: Routledge Classics, 2002.

Woodward, Ashley. *Nihilism in Postmodernity: Lyotard, Baudrillard, Vattimo*. Aurora: The Davies Group, 2009.

INDEX

The MIT Press Essential Knowledge Series

NOLEN GERTZ is Assistant Professor of Applied Philosophy at the University of Twente in the Netherlands.